Breaking and Training
the Driving Horse

A Detailed and Comprehensive Study

Second Edition Revised and Expanded

by
Doris L. Ganton

Published by
Melvin Powers
WILSHIRE BOOK COMPANY
12015 Sherman Road
No. Hollywood, California 91605
Telephone: (213) 875-1711 / (818) 983-1105

Printed by

HAL LEIGHTON PRINTING COMPANY
P.O. Box 3952
North Hollywood, California 91605
Telephone: (213) 983-1105

Printed in the United States of America
Library of Congress Catalog Card Number: 84-60805
ISBN 0-87980-272-3

In Memory of LUCKY

The best teacher and the truest friend
a horse could ever be.

FRONTISPIECE—H.R.H. The Duke of Edinburgh driving H.M. The Queen's winning team of Cleveland Bay horses in the Dressage section of the 1982 World Driving Championships at Windsor, England.
(With kind permission of H.R.H.) Photo by Horse and Driving.

Table of Contents

Page

Preface viii

Introduction x

Chapter One— Everyone Can Drive! 1
    Some Benefits from Driving
    From Nursery to Show Ring
    The Use of a Training Ring

Chapter Two— The Harness 3
    Functions
    Parts
    Definitions
    Adjustments
    Bitting Harness: Description and Uses

Chapter Three— Preparing the Green Colt for Driving 21
    Accustoming the Colt to Harness
    Lungeing
    Splint Boots
    Length of Lessons
    Ponying
    Introduction of Harness
    How to Hold the Reins
    Use of a Rein Board
    Gloves
    The Whip

Chapter Four— Starting the Green Colt in Harness 29
    Ground Driving
    Halts
    Using the Bitting Harness
    Driving Bridle with Blinkers
    Use of Traces as a Training Aid
    Breeching

Chapter Five— Work in Poles 35
    Poles: Design and Construction

Page

    Introduction of Poles
    Hitching the Colt in Poles

Chapter Six— Hitching in the Cart 43
    Type of Cart
    Familiarization
    Hitching the Colt in the Cart
    Work in the Cart
    Advanced Work in the Cart
    Backing Up
    Another Horse and Cart in the Ring
    Road Work and Obstacle Driving

Chapter Seven— Hitching in Four-Wheeled Buggy 51
    Precision Exercises
    Backing Up
    Advanced Work

Chapter Eight— Types of Vehicles and Harnesses 59
    Vehicles
    Buggies
    Care of Buggies
    Sleighing
    Harnesses
    Care of Harness

Chapter Nine— Hints and Happenings 65
    Hazards
    Driving Techniques
    Bits and Bitting
    Appointments and Attire
    Teams and Tandems
    Driving Outside the Ring

References 84

Index 85

LIST OF ILLUSTRATIONS

Figure   Page

1. Morgan Mare Harrowing IX
2. Singletree 4
3. Complete Harness 5
4. Parts of a Driving Bridle 6
5. Collar and Hames 8
6. Two Styles of Backpads 8
7. Crupper, Crupper Strap and Breeching 10
8. Driving Bridle 12
9. Tying up Traces 13
10. Wrap Straps 15
11. Correct Breeching Wrap 16
12. Bitting Harness 18
13. How to Hold Reins and Whip 25
14. A Rein Board 26
15. A Properly Fitted Bitting Harness 31
16. Use of Traces as a Training Aid 33
17. Construction of Poles 37
18. Driving in Poles 38
19. Cross-Country Cart 44
20. Driving in a Cart 47
21. Backing between Rails 52
22. Colt Hitched to a Four-Wheeled Buggy 53
23. Viceroy Show Buggy 55
24. Fine Harness Show Buggy 56
25. Road Wagon 57
26. Hackney Horse to a Viceroy 61
27. Arabian Formal Driving Horse 62
28. Roadster to a Caffrey Road Wagon 69
29. Pair Hackney Horses to a Ladies' Phaeton . . .70
30. Pair Morgan Horses 71
31. Pair Standardbred Roadsters 72
32. Some Driving Bits 67
33. Four-in-Hand of Hackney Horses 73
34. Tandem of Morgan Horses 74
35. Unicorn of Hackney Horses 75
36. Pleasure Driving Horse to a Ralli Car 77
37. Hackney Pony to a Basket Wicker Phaeton 78
38. Clydesdale Horse to an Antique Cart 82
39. HRH The Duke of Edinburgh 80
40. Six-Horse Hitch of Belgians 83

Preface

Many books have been written on the various aspects of riding and there appears to be an almost continuous flow of publications on the subject. As these are written for the most part by experts in their particular fields, the aspiring young rider has at his command an unlimited amount of information to help him in his training program. When it comes to the subject of DRIVING, however, the literary sources shrink to an unfortunate low — there are virtually no basic or detailed books to help the beginning driver. With the tremendous upswing in driving on this continent, the need for such a book has become increasingly evident.

The material for this book stems from my 30 years of experience with harness horses and from my notes developed in conjunction with the driving courses I have taught internationally for the past 15 years. Working with so many beginners has given me an insight into their problems, apprehensions, and requirements. Beginners share one wonderful quality—ENTHUSIASM! They want to learn to drive! This entire book is written with the aim of preserving and enhancing this quality as method and means are unfolded to the reader.

This book is written with the training of a colt in mind, but the instructions can just as easily be followed to train an older animal or a saddle horse to drive. In the case of a saddle horse (depending on his previous training and existing knowledge), many steps can be speeded up or even omitted, but basically the steps remain the same.

I wish to thank all the kind Whips who so generously contributed photographs for this new edition and Mrs. Carolyn Wheatcroft, whose artistic pen created the drawings contained in this book.

Figure 1. Morgan mare "Beckridge Nina" harrowing paddock. Owned and driven by Mrs. Ruth Laws, Victoria, B.C. (Light horses can do a lot of work around the farm.)

Introduction

Most of you are realizing only half the potential of your horses! If you are just riding your horse, you are only using a part of his ability. When a horse is trained to drive, his usefulness is vastly increased. He can be driven for pleasure on trails or country roads; he can pull a stoneboat hauling loads around the farm; he can double as the garden tractor pulling a cultivator. Tremendous enjoyment can be obtained as you take friends and elderly people along for rides through the countryside where, before, your saddle horse was limited to carrying you alone. If the show ring is your choice, your driving horse can, of course, perform in that capacity, adding extra classes to your ridden regime. He can also perform in the increasingly popular three-phase driving events where skill, stamina, ability and training combine to test your prowess. There is no end to the usefulness of a properly trained driving horse. A good driver is a thrill to watch and the art of driving is just as full of enjoyment, thrills and challenge as is riding.

Chapter One

Everyone Can Drive!

You can drive YOUR horse regardless of breed, type, age, or sex. The project may take varying lengths of time depending upon his temperament and disposition, but all horses CAN be driven. A quiet, even-tempered colt can usually be driving in the cart after three to four weeks of concentrated training. A fiery, high spirited, nervous animal may take twice that long or even longer. One must always progress at the horse's own speed, i.e. his ability to absorb and perform his lessons. The trainer must never exceed this ability or the results will be confusion, unpleasant resistance and a set-back in training. Horses as a rule are willing and co-operative as long as they can understand what it is that the trainer wants; therefore, it is necessary that communication be established on a level the horse can understand. Horses are creatures of habit, and repetition is the best teacher. If you bear this in mind as you go through the steps of teaching the horse to drive, you will find your task much easier.

All breeds of horses perform differently and have a distinct style of moving. Probably the most outstanding eye-catcher in the show ring is the Hackney. His fantastically high and snappy action portrays sheer elegance and rhythm. He is truly the aristocrat of the show ring! The American Saddlebred Fine Harness Horse is another of the ACTION horses. His erect carriage, brilliant action, and spirited way of going enhances one of the most thrilling classes at a show. Another breed with action is the Morgan Horse. These very versatile animals are at their best in harness and combine style and action with gentleness and manners. With a completely different but equally thrilling way of going is the Arabian Horse. The Arabian is noted for his breathtaking "floating" ex-

tension at the trot. With his gay tail carriage and classic dished face, his performance in the buggy is an experience that will become a lasting memory at any show. The Standardbred Horse is probably best known for his performance on the raceways in a racing sulky. He has incredible speed at a trot or pace, and a different way of going from the show horses. The Thoroughbred is another of the "low actioned" horses. He goes with a long, smooth striding trot in the buggy and has the ability to cover great distances with ease and speed. The Quarter Horse is a pleasure to use in harness because of his ease of handling. He, too, has a low going action and a much shorter stride at the trot than his relative, the Thoroughbred. The Appaloosa performs very well in harness for pleasure. His disposition makes him popular with beginners and his distinctive markings are attractive in the buggy. The various pony breeds are all ideal harness prospects. Ponies learn to drive very quickly, and because of their small stature are easier to handle in the initial stages of training. The Welsh Ponies and the Fine Harness type of Shetlands are smartly brilliant when in their harness turnouts and the cross-bred pleasure ponies make their usefulness known best in pony carts. Donkeys make excellent driving animals and are becoming increasingly popular in many areas. They are very docile, are not prone to nervousness, and are very easily trained. Unlike horses, they have an excellent sense of self-preservation and never allow themselves to be overworked, overfed or overcome by fright—a definite asset in the hands of beginners.

Some Benefits from Driving

Driving has another function—it is an excellent preliminary to saddle training. You can drive a young colt that would not be rideable for another year, and in doing so teach the colt many things. Driving teaches obedience, develops the colt's mouth to the point where he is actually "on the bit," develops his muscles, (especially his quarters) and strengthens any weakness that might be present in these areas. It muscles up his chest and legs, develops his head carriage, and teaches him to flex and bend. He learns a preliminary dressage movement in the crossing of his legs on the turns and in turns on the haunches. Above all, the colt learns to co-operate and work cheerfully with his trainer, which is the basis of all future training.

From Nursery to Show Ring

Most colts are ready to begin their training in harness at around two years of age. Some breeds are started earlier, depending upon the maturity the colt has attained. In this book, we will take the young colt from his quiet babyhood pasture to the excitement and drama of the show ring. The weeks of training will be hard work for both horse and trainer, but when carried out in a systematic and sensible manner will be very rewarding. Lessons can be very enjoyable when approached progressively, and the whole training process can become one that both trainer and horse look forward to every day. As the colt develops muscle, condition and knowledge, the lessons seem easier and when the difficult stages of training are reached, the colt is ready mentally and physically to cope with them.

The big secret in training a horse is to be able to recognize signs of boredom, confusion, or loss of interest. You must plan your lessons in a flexible timetable that allows adjustment to the horse's changing moods. Stopping a lesson at just the right time on a happy calm note does more for a horse's training than an extra hour of "trying to pound something into him." One must realize that physical resistance in a horse always goes hand-in-hand with mental resistance and while you may conquer physical resistance with brute force tactics, you still have the mental resistance to cope with.

The trainer's state of mind during these early training stages is even more important than that of the colt. Animals are very sensitive to a human's moods. The trainer must always radiate confidence and ability—regardless of his feelings. If he is really nervous and unsure of himself, he should not attempt to train a young horse.

Your colt's training begins in his stall where you gain his confidence and accustom him to your voice, presence, and handling. It continues on through work on the lunge line where he learns to do the various gaits on command and becomes conditioned to receiving and OBEYING orders. The introduction of the parts of the harness is accomplished in a gradual and interesting manner until he is wearing his full harness without realizing he is really doing anything out of the ordinary.

Ground driving is the next step and poses no problems to your colt as it occurs almost naturally in the course of his progressive lessons. When this becomes a normal and accepted part of his life, he is ready for the big transition to actual pulling. At the start and for some time he will pull "poles," a type of travois made out of two young green trees joined together near the rear. Being green, the poles are flexible and resilient, and, being young and small in diameter, are light and easy to pull. At this point, you are merely teaching the colt to accept the feel of SHAFTS on his sides and the slight pull on his chest. As he learns to drive freely in this travois, his lessons become more difficult and he learns to pull the poles in figures and increasingly tight corners. Once he is absolutely reliable in the poles, your colt is ready to be hitched to a two-wheeled cart. After some practice and advanced work in the cart, the colt can be safely hitched to a Show Buggy or any other type of four-wheeled vehicle. In this manner, you end up with a happy, calm, well-educated driving horse who thoroughly understands his work and enjoys it.

Use of a Training Ring

This book has been written with instructions referring to the use of a training ring. Lest the reader think a proper training ring is absolutely essential to the training of a driving horse, let me clarify the situation.

The availability and use of a training ring is a great advantage and a desirable asset, but is not an absolute necessity. Any contained area ranging from 60×100 to 100×200 feet will do the same job. It IS advisable to have it contained (or fenced, if you wish) for the sake of safety and concentration. A horse keeps his mind on his work far better if he knows he is in an enclosed area, whereas in a big open field he is subjected to too many ideas and influences. Good footing is essential, and the training ring usually provides this advantage. If you are working on grass, the corners are liable to be slippery and the time of day will affect the condition as well. A colt in training has enough to worry about without having to worry about his footing, so if you train off grass, choose the time of day when it is driest. The training ring at home also conditions and prepares the colt for the show ring and, with its soft texture, eliminates any worries over leg troubles occurring from pounding on hard surfaces.

Chapter Two

The Harness

Functions

The driving harness has three functions: pulling, stopping, and controlling the horse.

The horse pulls the load by pushing against the breastcollar. The breastcollar is a fairly wide strap that goes around the horse's chest. The pull is transferred to the cart by traces attached to the singletree. The traces are long and fairly narrow straps connected to the breastcollar that lie along the horse's sides from chest to flank. The singletree is the wooden bar on the cart, running from shaft to shaft above the crossbar, and pivoted in the middle to allow it to swing in step with the horse's shoulders (see Figure 2).

The horse stops the load by the use of wrap straps or breeching. The wrap straps wrap around the shaft, securing the shaft loops at a fixed point and effecting a halt through the backpad and crupper when the horse stops (see Figure 10). The breeching goes around the horse's flanks and is attached to the shafts by breeching straps (see Figure 11). The halt is effected by the horse bracing himself with his quarters against this strap, thus stopping the load.

The horse is steered and stopped by long reins running from his bit to the driver's hands, and is assisted by the checkrein (uphaul) and martingale (downhaul) (see Figure 3).

Parts of Harness and Their Definitions

Starting at the horse's head and working back, I shall identify the parts of the harness in the order in which they are found. Harness for the most part is a simple affair, and the various parts are usually named after the location in which they are used, i.e. the "backpad" is used on the horse's back.

The Driving Bridle

This bridle consists of cheekstraps and crown as in an ordinary riding bridle, PLUS the blinkers and the checkrein. The blinkers are situated on the cheekstraps and shield the eye area. Blinkers may be either square or round. The checkrein can be one of two types: overdraw or side-checking. The overdraw checkrein goes from the bit, up the front of the horse's head between his ears and on down his neck on top of his mane to a hook on the packpad. The proper name for this hook is water hook. The side-checking type goes from each side of the bit, up behind the cheekstraps, and though a drop from the crown below the horse's ears to the hook on the backpad. The bit is usually a half-cheek snaffle, either jointed or straight, depending on which type of bit works best with your horse. The half-cheek on the ends of the bit keeps it from being pulled through the horse's mouth and also helps to balance it in his mouth. Often a noseband is added to the driving bridle. This, when properly adjusted, keeps the horse's mouth closed, thus giving the driver more control.

The Breastcollar

The breastcollar and traces are the means by which the horse pulls the vehicle. The thickness and width vary greatly depending upon the type of work being contemplated. The traces are either sewn onto the breastcollar and have horizontal holes on the other end for attaching to the singletree, or are buckled on with the adjustment at the billet end via the buckle.

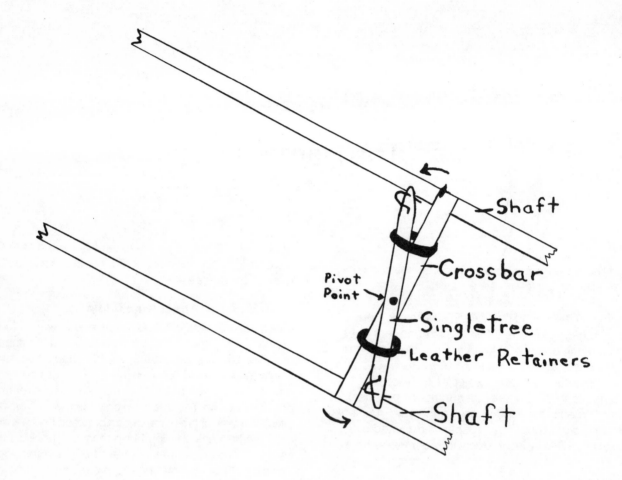

Figure 2. Singletree

THE HARNESS

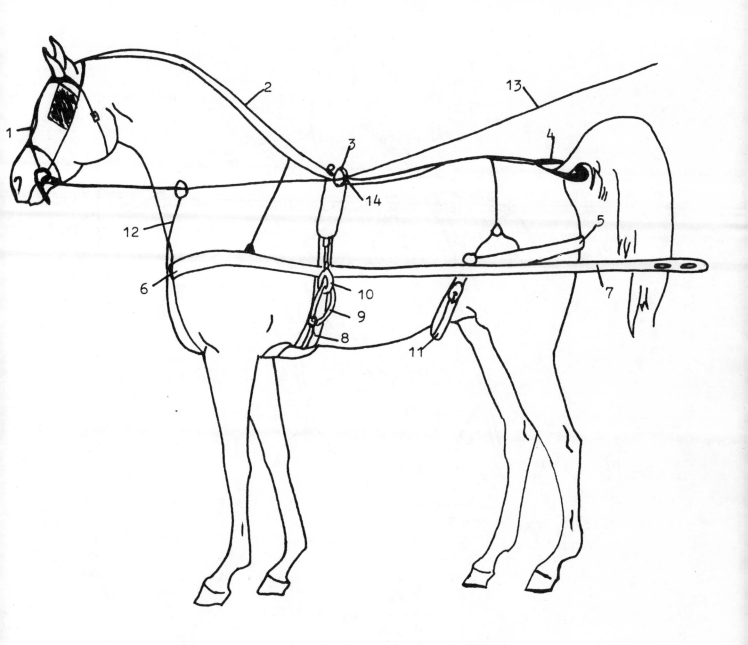

1. Bridle
2. Checkrein
3. Backpad
4. Crupper
5. Breeching
6. Breastcollar
7. Trace

8. Surcingle
9. Wrap Strap
10. Shaft Loop
11. Breeching Strap
12. Running Martingale
13. Rein
14. Ring (or Rein) Terret

Figure 3. Complete Harness

5

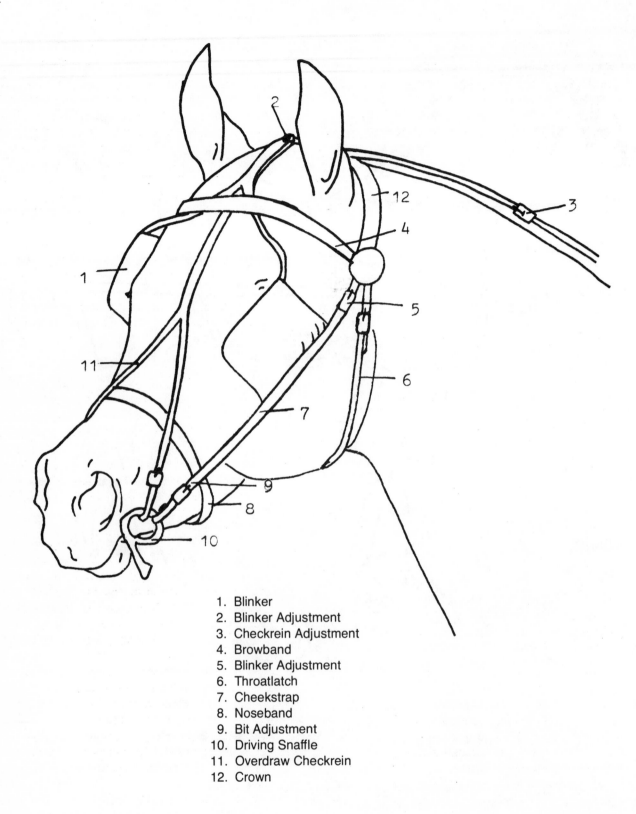

1. Blinker
2. Blinker Adjustment
3. Checkrein Adjustment
4. Browband
5. Blinker Adjustment
6. Throatlatch
7. Cheekstrap
8. Noseband
9. Bit Adjustment
10. Driving Snaffle
11. Overdraw Checkrein
12. Crown

Figure 4. Parts of a Driving Bridle

Collar and Hames

The use of collar and hames to pull the load instead of a breastcollar is more common overseas than on this continent with respect to driving a single horse. The collar goes around the horse's neck, lying along the shoulder groove. The hames—two half-round shaped pieces of metal—fit snugly in the hame groove of the collar, and are held together top and bottom by hame straps (see Figure 5). It is very important that the collar fit the horse perfectly and as collars are scarce in most areas, breastcollar style is much more practical. With the collar in position on the horse, one should be able to insert a closed fist between the collar and the horse's neck. He should also be able to put his fingers under the rim on the sides of the horse's neck. Too large a collar is almost as dangerous to a horse as a too small one. Every horse must have his own well-fitted collar and hames as every horse's neck shape is different. The traces buckle onto the hame tugs, which are attached to lugs on the hames at the point of draft and are adjustable at the buckle end.

To measure a collar, the distance between the ends (inside, lengthwise) gives the size, i.e. 20″, 20½″ etc. To measure a horse for a collar, put a carpenter's square along the horse's shoulder with the short end under his neck at the chest, and the other—long end—at the withers. Hold a carpenter's level across the withers and read off the length on the square. Add half an inch to allow some room. If you are planning to pull really heavy loads, collar and hames style harness is a necessity.

The Backpad or Saddle

The backpad sits on the horse's back about two inches behind the withers and consists of the pad itself and two ring terrets for the reins. It has shaft loops, one on either side hung from dee rings, and a bellyband or surcingle to secure it on the horse. Attached to the bellyband are wrap straps—narrow straps about three feet long that wrap around the shafts and effect the braking force. The backpad also has the water hook on the top at center front.

The Crupper

The crupper is a stuffed and rounded piece of leather that goes under the horse's tail and is connected to the backpad by the crupper strap, or backstrap as it is sometimes called. It is either sewn or buckled to the crupper strap. The leather in the crupper is always very soft and pliable as this is a very sensitive and vulnerable area on the horse.

The Breeching

The breeching is the means by which the horse stops the vehicle. The breeching goes around the horse's rear quarters and is held up by a loin strap that goes through a slot in the backstrap. It is connected to the shafts on each side by means of breeching straps. These straps go from the rings on either end of the breeching to the metal fitting (footman loop) on the underside of the shaft, designed for that purpose. The strap then wraps around the shaft in the manner shown by Figure 11. Figure 7 shows a complete breeching, crupper and crupper strap.

Adjustment Of Harness

Every part of the harness serves a specific purpose, and the fit and adjustment of each part is extremely important. Many a horse is scalded or rubbed by an ill-fitting harness and turns sour and difficult because of the discomfort and pain. Always make sure that your horse's harness is fitted and done up properly before moving off in a lesson. This ensures that the colt will be able to devote his attention to the lesson instead of to the discomfort of badly adjusted equipment.

Blinkers

People often wonder why blinkers are worn. The main reason is to prevent the horse from seeing activity around him, *especially* behind him, and becoming frightened. Blinkers concentrate the horse's attention on the work in front of him. They keep his mind on the driver's instructions and prevent him from being distracted by his surroundings. This is especially important out on the road and also in the show ring where distractions and frightening sights are numerous.

The adjustment of a driving bridle can be bewildering to the beginner due to the number of pieces attached to it (see Figure 4). First, adjust the length of the cheekstrap so that the bit lies in the proper position in the colt's mouth. The proper position is high up so that the horse cannot get his tongue over the bit. The very bottom buckle, below the cheekstrap tube, is the ONLY adjustment for length. The buckle at the top of the cheekstrap just below his ear is for adjusting the blinker, and it is for that purpose only. It should never be used to adjust the bridle. The eye should be centered on the inside of the blinker and the buckle immediately above the blinker on the cheekstrap used for raising or lowering its height. There is a further adjustment for the blinkers that allows them to be pulled in closer to the head. It is done by tightening the narrow strap running from the tips of the blinkers to the buckle on the top center of the crown. The blinkers should be facing almost straight ahead. They should not be loose enough to allow them to slant outwards and should not be tight enough to make them rest against the horse's eye. Depending upon the breed of horse and his ensuing conformation, the blinkers will sit

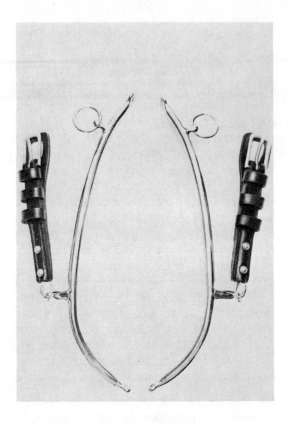

Figure 5. Collar and Hames. Collar of Kay Style; Hames with Hame Tugs attached.

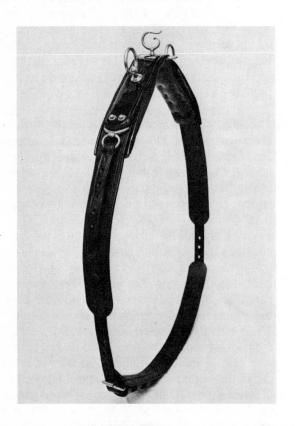
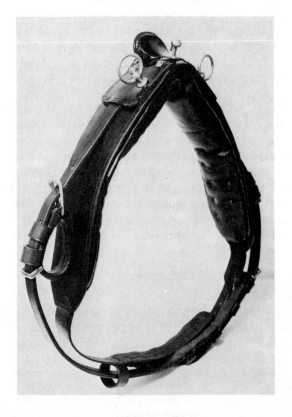

Figure 6. Two Styles of Backpads. Left: a light show or pleasure style. Right: a Gig Harness Style with sliding tugs (shaft loops).

on different angles, some wider than others. It is more comfortable for the horse if you clip off the long guard hairs that grow immediately above and below the eye. If these hairs are left on, they will constantly brush against the blinkers, often causing a horse to shake his head or throw it. The cheekstrap must also be adjusted carefully so that when the checkrein is on and pulling upwards on the bit the cheekstrap does not become slack and flop outwards. If this happens the horse can see to the rear, a potentially frightening experience that could lead to a runaway.

Horses have considerable vision to the rear due to the placement of their eyes. A flopping cheekstrap allows them to see just enough to become alarmed. It is for this reason that one must NEVER take the bridle off while the horse is hitched to a vehicle. This seemingly innocuous act has caused innumerable bad accidents and runaways. A horse becomes frightened when he sees something coming behind him that is attached to HIM, so you must be careful to adjust your bridle to cut off all vision to the rear. Horses are required to wear blinkers in the show ring, and, for reasons of safety as well as control, ought not to be driven anywhere without them.

The Checkrein

The main purpose of the checkrein is to keep the horse's head in a more or less fixed position in the perpendicular plane. This position varies with the stage of training, the type of work you are doing, and the conformation of the horse, but the horse should always have a checkrein on. If a horse cannot get his head down he can't kick hard. You can easily see the reasons for this by looking at the anatomy of a horse. With the checkrein making it impossible for him to get his head down, he usually doesn't think of kicking because he associates that act with having his head down. With his head in position, you are gaining much greater control due to the fact that the bit will be resting on the bars of his mouth.

The checkrein has been called many cruel things. Most people think of *Black Beauty* when checkreins are mentioned, but, of course, this was a unique case. Use of checkreins is NOT cruel unless you make it so. They ARE the means by which you control your horse to a great extent, and many times your safety depends upon having your checkrein in the proper position. The type of checkrein will vary depending upon your horse's conformation and whether you are planning to show your horse or to drive purely for pleasure. A side check tends to set a horse's head easier and is more comfortable for most horses, but is not allowed on certain breeds in the show ring. Use of a checkrein assists the balance of a horse and encourages them to use their rear quarters with better engagement.

The Running Martingale

The running martingale is used in conjunction with an overdraw checkrein. It is a narrow strap that runs from the center of the bellyband, up the chest, through the tab on the breastcollar, and forks into two straps ending in rings through which the reins pass enroute to the bit (see Figure 3). While the checkrein prevents the horse's head from lowering, the running martingale prevents the head from being carried too high. You cannot control a horse that has his head straight in the air. The action of the checkrein and martingale together gives the driver the utmost control and ease of handling as it keeps the bit in exactly the proper spot in the mouth. The martingale also allows the driver to exert tremendous force upon the mouth should it be required. The martingale should be adjusted so that it is not in play at all when the horse's head is in the proper position. When the rein is correctly adjusted, it should be a straight line from the bit to the rein terret, through the rings of the martingale. It should not have a big dip or "vee" in it at the martingale rings. Only if the horse throws his head above this point does it exert a downward force. If you use an overdraw checkrein, you also should use a running martingale for utmost safety and control. This combination has a very steadying effect on a horse and he comes to depend on it to a certain extent.

A running martingale can be used with sidechecks in the training stages but is not customarily used this way in the show ring. If for some reason you have your horse bitted down in one of the curb positions of a Liverpool or similar curb bit, a running martingale should never be used. It applies far too much force in this mode.

Breastcollar and Traces

As the breastcollar and traces are the means by which the horse pulls the load, it is evident they must fit properly and be in the right place to make pulling possible. The height of the breastcollar on the horse's chest is quite important. It should lie at the base of his neck, on his chest. It must not be up on his neck to restrict his breathing nor must it be down near the point of his shoulders to rub and scald him. A horse's shoulders move one at a time and this means that the breastcollar is always moving on his chest. It must be in the proper place to avoid rubbing him and it must be kept exceedingly clean to avoid a gall or scald (see Figures 16 and 22 for correct position).

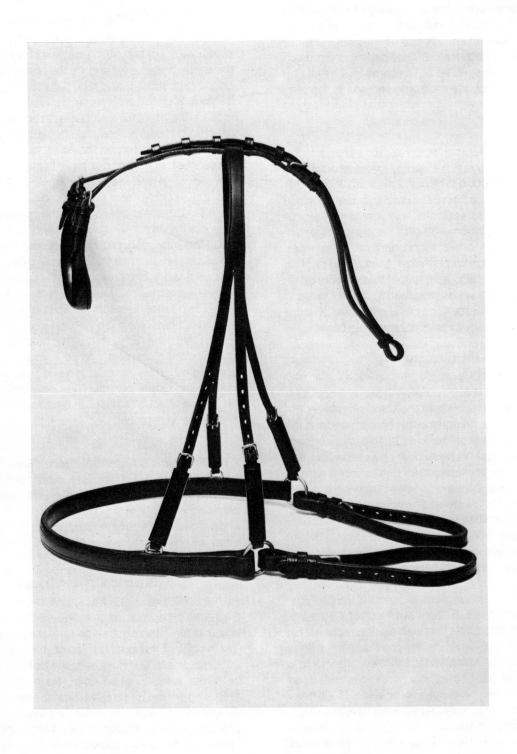

Figure 7. Crupper, crupper strap and Breeching.

The use of a breastcollar pad is a good idea. These pads are readily available at harness tack shops, and are made of soft polyester, furry material and have handy Velcro tab closures for quick and easy attachment. They make the breastcollar more comfortable for the horse and save the harness leather. Being washable, it is convenient to clean them in the washing machine often, thus accomplishing three things—keep the leather clean, assure the horse's comfort, and keep the pads clean.

The breastcollar is connected by the traces directly to the singletree. The singletree pivots at its center which allows the movement of the shoulders to be absorbed and transformed into forward motion. The height of the breastcollar is adjusted by the neck strap, a narrow strap that goes over the horse's neck, and buckles onto each side of the breastcollar.

The traces should lie in line with the shafts when the horse is hitched to a vehicle. To effect this, do not change the height of the traces—change the height of the shafts. This is done by lowering or raising the shaft loops on the backpad. The position of the traces is fixed by the breastcollar and cannot be changed, so always change the height of the shafts to achieve neat and clean horizontal lines.

When not in use, the traces should be tied up. This keeps them from being stepped on and possibly broken and also, when tied properly, keeps the leather in good shape without kinks or twists. Double the free end back up underneath to the place where it joins the breastcollar. Holding the now doubled trace in your left hand up close to the breastcollar, pass the other end of the trace over the held end from right to left—twice—then pass the end back through the first loop (see Figure 9). This creates a neat and secure wrap which will stay put even as you lunge the horse. Always take the few seconds required to tie up the traces before you take the horse out of the shafts. This can prevent problems arising from loose traces falling down, being stepped on, or flopping around and spooking a horse at a critical moment.

The Backpad or Saddle

The backpad sits about 2 inches behind the withers on the horse's back. Its only means of adjustment is by the bellyband or surcingle, and this is done up fairly snugly but not tight. It should never be as tight as the girth on a riding saddle. It is a narrow strap and you could easily hurt a horse by tightening it too much. It doesn't need to be tight as its sole purpose is to provide a base for the rein terrets and shaft loops. Suspended from the back-

pad on either side are the shaft loops or shaft holders. Their adjustment is by their hangers, and as mentioned above, they are lowered or raised to allow the shafts to lie in line with the traces.

A polyester pad under the backpad is a good idea for the same reasons given regarding the breastcollar pads. These usually come in pairs. As they also come in many colors, one can match them with their cart or driving attire. They can brighten up a very old or drab harness.

Sometimes it is impossible to have the shafts and traces in line due to the construction of the vehicle. Some carts are built very low to the ground which, if the horse is tall, results in the shafts sloping upwards at a considerable angle. In such a case, the shafts and traces cannot lie in a parallel plane with the horse's topline nor with each other.

The balance of the cart is very important. The load should be arranged so it is not overbalanced to the rear. This would result in a constant pull upwards on the bellyband and cause great strain and irritation to the horse. The balance of the cart should be such that NO upward pull is exerted on the horse's middle and a slight downward force is established. This force helps the horse maintain his balance as he pulls the load and assists him in keeping a steady gait. The cart should also be in proportion to the horse or pony.

Wrap Straps

Wrap straps are sometimes called the second bellyband as they go around the horse's girth on top of the surcingle. These wrap straps wrap around the shafts, securing the shaft loop firmly against the stop on the shaft, and act as BRAKES when you ask the horse to stop. The wrap strap should be brought up on the inside of the trace (next to the horse) and wrapped over the shaft in front of the shaft loop; around underneath and figure-eighted behind the shaft loop and the stop; then buckled up tightly on the outside of the trace (see Figure 10). The trace should always be between any connecting straps such as wrap straps or breeching straps. The trace should never be wrapped up by the wrap straps, just trapped in between. This method helps hold the trace in place and presents a neat appearance. Both sides of the wrap straps should be even if possible, i.e. if you have one wrap front and rear of the shaft loop on one side of the horse, you should have the same on the other side. You should try to keep things as symmetrical as possible when harnessing a horse. When the wrap straps are buckled in position, you may find that the bellyband has become loose. So always check this and, if necessary,

Figure 8. Driving Bridle with overdraw checkrein and square blinkers, properly fitted.

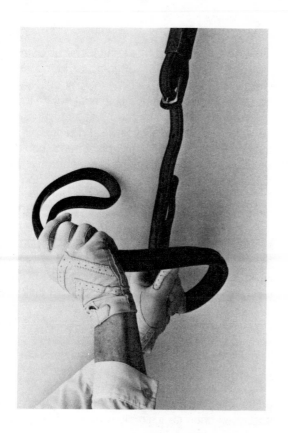
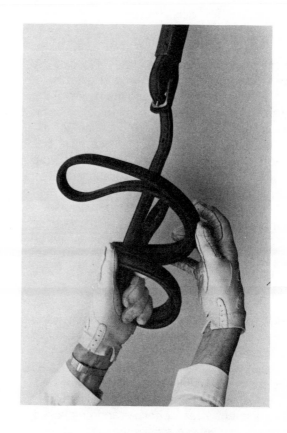

Figure 9. Correct Method of Tying up Traces.

tighten it up a hole before moving on. It must be remembered that the purpose of the wrap straps is to keep the shafts from flopping up and down and to establish a solid connection for use in controlling the speed of the cart. They should never be used to tighten up the backpad. A horse's back could be scalded or hurt through the use of too tight wrap straps, and a pressure point created if used for any length of time. Similarly, if wrap straps are too tight, they can cause pressure sores on your horse's back at the point where the dee rings supporting the shaft hangers come out of the backpad. A white hair growth is produced in a small area where the pressure was applied. This is very painful for the horse and, trying to combat this discomfort, could cause him to act up in some way. One sees the same effect from ill-fitting riding saddles.

The STOPS on the shafts mentioned above consist of small metal protrusions from the shaft, about 14 inches from its tip. Their function is to give the shaft loops a solid surface to push against to prevent them freely sliding back on the shafts when braking is desired. Some buggies have several stops spaced about two inches apart for use with different sizes of horses and harnesses. They also dress up a vehicle as they are made of solid, shiny brass.

The Crupper

The crupper is connected to the backpad by the crupper strap. The reason for having a crupper on a harness is to hold the backpad in position and not allow it to be pulled up on the withers by the force on the checkrein. Therefore, the crupper must fit fairly snugly under the tail. Adjust the crupper strap so that the crupper hangs about one-half inch below the dock. This means that when the horse moves forward, the tail will come up even further off the crupper giving it sufficient clearance. A too tight crupper will gall the very soft underside of the horse's tail and cause him great discomfort, even making him "crupper shy" if its use is continued long enough. On the other hand, a too loose crupper allows the crupper strap to flop from side to side across the croup, destroying its usefulness and creating an unsightly and untidy harnessing job. A crupper must be kept very clean and soft, and a good driver gets into the habit of examining it every time he removes a set of harness. A dirty crupper will sore a horse quickly and this can lead to tail switching, bucking, or kicking—which we can easily do without in our driving endeavors.

The Breeching

A very effective means of stopping the vehicle is by the use of breeching which fits around the horse's rear quarters and is fastened to the shafts. The adjustment of the breeching is done by tightening or loosening the loin strap over the croup. The breeching should lie on the flat part of the horse's rear flank. It must not be too high or it will slide upwards under the horse's tail, and it must not be too low or it will slip down and pinch him near the gaskin. Either of these maladjustments could cause a kicking spree. The breeching is connected to breeching straps on either side, which in turn wrap round the shafts through metal fittings. These fittings, for use with a medium-sized horse, should be about 50 inches forward of the singletree and on the underside of the shaft. The breeching straps should be just slack enough to allow about one inch of play when the horse is moving forward. You do not want the breeching to be so tight that it is always rubbing on the horse; it should only come into strong contact when stopping. If you have too much slack in the breeching straps, your stops will be erratic and the buggy will roll forward a bit before the breeching "catches." This is hard on the harness and very irritating to the horse. The method of wrapping the breeching straps around the shafts requires a bit of finesse to achieve a neat and efficient look, but with a bit of practice it can become a simple procedure (see Figure 11). Thread the end of the breeching strap through the metal fitting (footman loop) under the shaft and wrap it TOWARDS the front of the horse over the first part of the strap. Wrap around three or four times (depending upon how much strap you have to spare), keeping the wraps loose. Then thread the free end underneath the wraps on TOP of the shaft, pull the whole bit up snugly, and buckle it back onto the breeching part. Now both ends come out of the neat wrapped fitting and everything remains flat and tidy. Do *not* wrap the trace—just trap it in between.

There are two other types of breeching that can be used with single harness. The first consists of a strong strap that runs from one trace buckle around the horse's quarters to the other trace buckle. This method is quick and easy to put on and requires no extra fittings on the cart or harness. It is held up at the quarters by a hanger over the croup, in the same manner as the breeching described above. Instead of buckling through footman loops under the shafts, the breeching straps—usually the same width as the traces—buckle into the same buckle as the trace at the breastcollar. I have never had as much confidence in this method as the conventional type that fastens to the shafts. This method works only when a buckle-on style of breastcollar/traces is used.

The second type of breeching is simply a broad strap stretched tautly across the shafts about 10 inches in

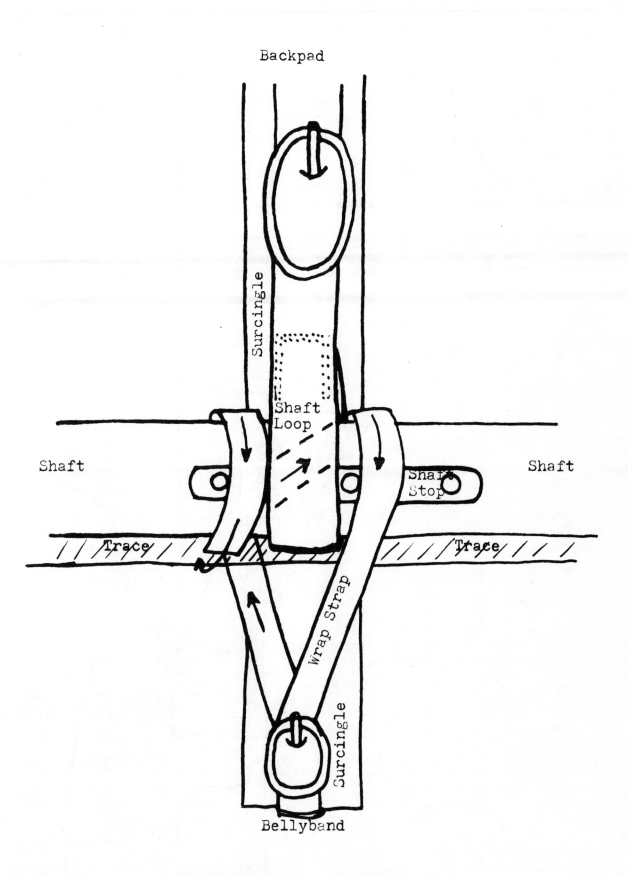

Figure 10. Proper Wrap for Wrap Straps.

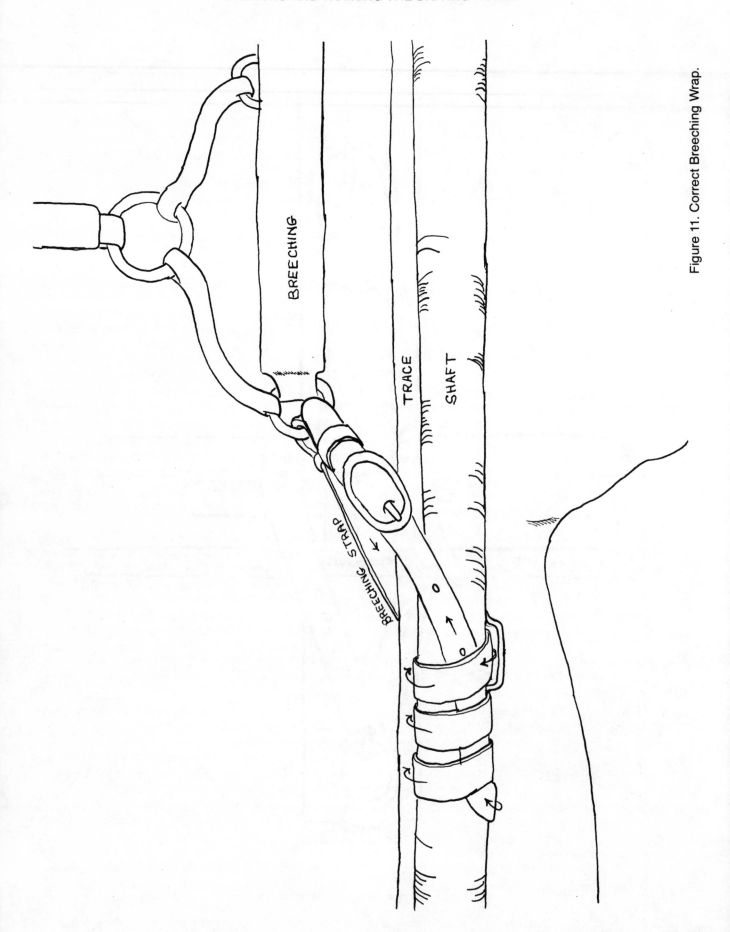

BREECHING

BREECHING STRAP

TRACE

SHAFT

Figure 11. Correct Breeching Wrap.

front of the crossbar of the cart. This type is always ready and requires no putting-on or taking-off as it is left on the shafts at all times. It requires no adjustments and is neat in appearance. This method of stopping the cart is known as "Brown's Patent." It puts the breeching strap in a very low position on most horses, which could lead to a problem occasionally with touchy horses, and is not suitable for constant use.

When pulling heavy loads, breeching MUST be used. It is the only fair way for both horse and harness. Also, if negotiating rough and hilly country even with light loads, breeching makes it much easier on the horse. He will tire less easily and the wear and tear on both harness and cart will be reduced considerably. However, breeching is seldom used in the show ring and is unnecessary for light carts and show buggies on normal level terrain.

Kicking Strap

A kicking strap is used on single harness to discourage a horse that is inclined to kick. This device consists of a strong strap that runs from shaft to shaft, up over the croup of the horse right in front of the crupper. It is held in place by a loop on the crupper strap. It should be adjusted so that it will not grab the horse unless he kicks, i.e. if he inadvertently breaks into a canter it should allow room for the movement of his quarters. Most of our modern horses do not have kicking tendencies and the kicking strap is seldom seen any more; however, it is an extremely useful item of equipment to have in the tack room. There are several other styles of kicking straps, but none that are as easily and safely applied as this one. One style that is definitely to be avoided is the kind that goes from the horse's bit to a small rope under his tail — a horse can be made extremely sore and crupper-shy for the rest of his life by such an inhumane method.

Bitting Harness

Description and Uses

The bitting harness is a tremendously useful piece of equipment for the training of both colts and older animals. It consists of an open bridle with side checks and side reins, backpad and bellyband, crupper and stay-straps (see Figure 12). Its advantage over the driving harness is the presence of the side reins and stay straps. The side reins run from a dee ring on the side of the backpad to the bit, and can be adjusted in both length and height. They restrict the movement in a lateral manner, i.e. from side to side, and when used in conjunction with the side checks (checkrein) maintain the horse's head in any position the trainer chooses. Naturally, when used on a young colt

both of these reins are quite loose at the beginning and are adjusted as required.

The backpad on a bitting harness is a heavily padded, wide, thick piece of leather to which are attached several dee rings and round rings to allow the training aids to be used in a wide range of positions. It has a wide, padded, comfortable bellyband with large and easily done-up buckles. The crupper strap is attached to the back of the backpad as in the driving harness, but the crupper strap on the bitting harness has two additional straps attached to it, one on each side running from a triangularly shaped piece of leather on top of the croup on an angle to the lower side of the backpad. This secures the crupper more firmly in place, preventing entirely any side-to-side motion of the crupper strap, and in addition holds the backpad in position at the point where the side reins are attached. With the pull being exerted forwards by the horse's mouth (bit), the backpad is inclined to move forward onto the horse's elbows where it could cause pain and swelling after a time. Not only would it be painful, but it would teach the horse that he *could* pull the reins out of your hands. This leads to the all-too-common bad habit of "snatching" as the horse walks. It is very uncomfortable and tiring for the driver and a habit that is difficult to cure. The *stay straps* just described prevent this from occurring and steady the entire harness.

The bit must be a straight bar, half cheek snaffle. Tremendous pressure can be exerted upon the horse's mouth via the side reins and side checks. If a jointed bit is used, the horse never gets relief (i.e. reward) from it when he gives (flexes) to it, as it just pinches the corners of his mouth. So eventually he just lies on the bit and develops a hard mouth and a resistance to all our efforts. With a straight bar, the moment he does the right thing, i.e. gives, he gets instant relief, so naturally he tries to achieve relief and learns to give to our hands. A curb bit should NOT be used in a bitting harness.

The backpad also has rings through which we can run our long reins and drive the colt from the ground. Therefore, this bitting harness can be employed for all the basic steps of training right up to the point where the driving bridle with blinkers is introduced, and it certainly saves your good harness. The bitting harness also plays a big part in achieving good head carriage and is a marvelous way to handle wild or unruly animals with safety and ease.

The adjustment of the bitting harness is just as critical as that of the driving harness. The side reins, for instance,

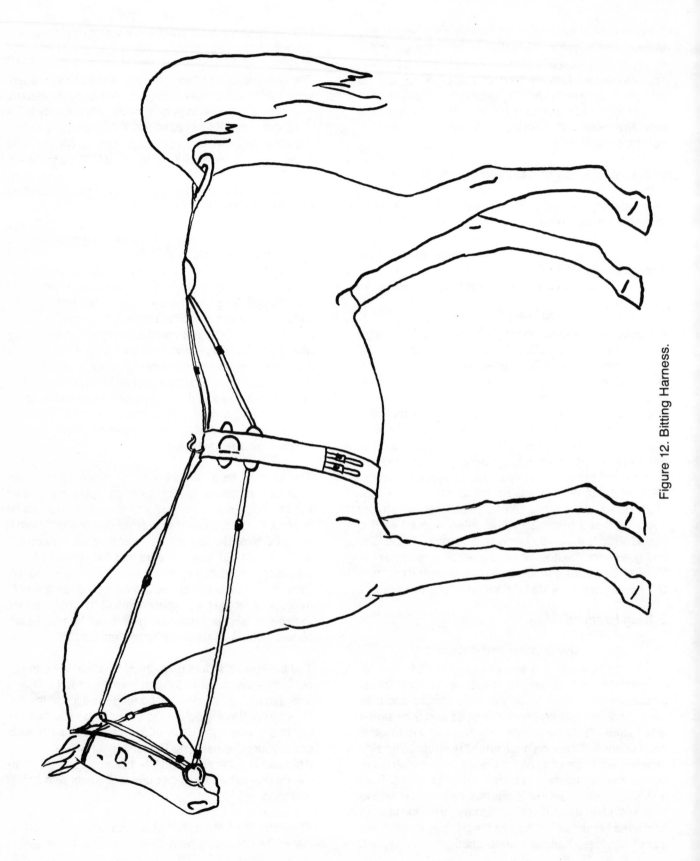

Figure 12. Bitting Harness.

must be carefully adjusted for length according to the stage of training, the knowledge of the horse, and the size of the animal. At the beginning, they should only be tight enough to prevent the horse from throwing his head from side to side. These reins can be most severe and cause much damage to a horse's mouth, carriage, and disposition. They must be of a length suitable for the work at hand, and must never in any case be left on for any length of time. Apart from the stay straps on the crupper strap, the rest of the bitting harness is adjusted in the same manner as the driving harness already described. The stay straps are made tight enough to prevent the backpad from slipping forward on to the elbows. Figure 15 shows a properly fitted Bitting Harness with a good view of stay straps doing their job correctly.

Chapter Three

Preparing The Green Colt For Driving

Accustoming the colt to harness

For our purpose I shall suppose that you have a young green colt, about two years old, well halter-broken and accustomed to being handled and led about. To prepare him for the crupper, there are a couple of exercises we can do (from foalhood on) that will make the crupper less of a surprise or shock when it is introduced. As we work around him, stand beside his flank opposite his tail and lift his tail with one hand. Lay your other arm across his buttocks under his tail, up near the tail head and gently let the tail down on your forearm. Reassure the colt, lift the tail off your arm, let it down again and repeat a few times each time you work around the colt. Very soon he will accept this situation without any reaction. Next wrap a 1½-inch wooden dowel, or a short length of an old handle off a rake or fork, with something soft and use this instead of your forearm under his tail, still braced across his buttocks. With this simple preparation, the crupper should present no problem.

To prepare the colt for the sight and feel of harness being thrown over his back and other places, use a saddle blanket or a big towel to kind of sack him out. Let the colt sniff and check the towel, then gradually start rubbing him all over with it, working up to gently slapping him with it and finally throwing it over his neck, back, croup, etc. NEVER throw it over his head, nor slap him on the head with anything; this could easily make him head shy. Work from both sides with the towel or blanket so that the colt becomes accustomed to it.

Lungeing

Before any harness or saddle training can begin, the colt must be taught to lunge. There are many excellent books on this subject (Ref. 1) and lungeing is an art in itself. I cannot begin to give a comprehensive account of lungeing in this short chapter, but a very simplified version would go as follows: The object of lungeing is to have the horse go around in a large circle with you at the center holding the lunge line (a leather or webbing line, usually about 25 feet in length). Instead of turning on the spot at the center, it is often more advantageous to walk a small circle (perhaps six feet in diameter), thus encouraging the colt to move on while maintaining his attention. The horse is made to walk, trot, canter, and stop on the lungeing circle from commands given both orally and with the assistance of the lunge line. He must be able to do these gaits either way, i.e. to both left and right on command. A lungeing whip is usually carried by the trainer and this helps reinforce his commands and prevents the horse from coming into the center of the circle or reversing direction. I prefer to teach a horse to obey verbal commands on the lunge line for several reasons. Because a horse is able to learn the meaning of the words "walk," "trot" and "whoa" very easily, the trainer does not have to spend any extra time teaching these words while he teaches the colt to lunge. As communication is the most important factor in training the horse, the fact that he knows and understands the basic words you require of him is of great assistance in keeping him calm and less confused by additional things you are asking of him. In an emergency situation, such as a rein breaking or a tangle of some sort, you can command WHOA and expect your horse to halt immediately because of his ingrained reflex training to the verbal command.

Once your colt has learned voice commands and is lungeing satisfactorily on a lunge line, it is of considerable advantage to "free lunge" him. This requires a fenced round ring about 65–70 feet in diameter. As no lunge line is used, it is of paramount importance that the colt understands and obeys verbal commands. Free lungeing promotes better balance, bending, and obedience. With no lunge line to lean on or pull out against, the colt must find his own balance on his feet and will soon find it easier to bend into the circle to achieve this. He is usually more attentive to the trainer's presence and commands, and it is a real thrill to have the "free" colt start, stop, and perform the gaits asked for strictly on voice commands. Because he is free, the colt usually performs with more vigor and eagerness, showing us potential and capabilities of which we may have been unaware. It is wise to intersperse free lungeing with work on the lunge line to reaffirm your mastery of the colt and to correct any problems.

As well as being trained on the lunge line, your green colt must be accustomed to wearing a bit in his mouth. This is best accomplished by using a MOUTHING BIT, a soft snaffle with dangling "keys" which encourage the colt to play with it. This bit is usually attached by small snaps to his halter and he should be made to wear it for an hour or so at a time. Let him eat his hay with it on, and he will become used to the feel of it very quickly. Adjust this bit just as carefully as a driving bit or riding bit. It must not hang down in his mouth where he might be able to get his tongue over it. Getting the tongue over the bit is a very difficult habit to break once a horse has learned it, but it must never be tight enough to cause pain or actual discomfort. Remember that the colt will have to wear and respect a bit for the rest of his life, and his first impressions will be lasting ones. If a mouthing bit is not available, an adequate substitute can be easily made using a straight bar, half cheek snaffle with a curb chain wound around it and secured at each end.

Once you have your young, and not-quite-so-green, colt lungeing calmly and happily both ways of the circle, changing gaits upon command, and accustomed and content to carry a bit in his mouth, you are ready to begin his training in harness.

Splint Boots

Youngsters, being green, impetuous, and a bit awkward, are prone to hit themselves and bang their legs occasionally. For this and other reasons, I like to wear splint boots for all my training. I prefer the type that cover the ankle (fetlock joint) as well as the cannon bone and have a vertically raised soft strip that sits over the splint bone. The best buy is the style with double Velcro closures for ease of putting-on and removing. Splint boots are also

invaluable when driving out on the roads as they help to absorb some of the concussion and give support to the lower leg. They are useful on a horse of any age driven in this manner. It is not usually necessary to wear boots on the hind legs.

Length of Lessons

The length of lessons must vary with the concentration span and type of work. At first, the colt will have a very short span, and being unaccustomed to any of this training will tire quickly. Your lesson should always end before the colt tires or gets bored. At the beginning, I like to give two short lessons a day, each of about 15 minutes duration, one in the morning and one in the afternoon. It means a lot more bother and work, but in the long run produces a far better animal. Two short lessons are far more valuable than one long lesson. The colt is fresh and eager and has had time to digest the previous lessons. Horses learn mainly by repetition and habit, and frequent lessons involving putting-on and taking-off of harness soon become an ingrained habit and a part of his life. As the colt progresses and becomes stronger, so the lessons may become longer. I have found two half-hour lessons a day to be the most productive and successful.

Always start and end lessons with something the colt knows well and can do easily. This puts the colt in the right frame of mind to continue the lesson and leaves him in a happy and contented mood afterwards. Also, if trouble arises at any stage of training, always return to some exercise the colt understands and can do. The trouble likely was caused by a communication problem and, rather than excite or fight with the colt, immediately ask him to do something else. Then, consider the problem and decide how best to solve it.

If ever you have a fight with your colt, you MUST win! If the colt flagrantly disobeys a command that you know he understands, make him execute the command immediately. Always strive to avoid provoking a fight, but if one ensues, enforce your command by whatever means necessary.

Ponying

It is a welcome change of scenery and pace to pony (lead from horseback) your colt occasionally. You must ride a quiet, well-trained horse and one not prone to kicking at another horse bumping into it. Use a longer-than-usual lead shank—about ten feet—so that you have length to control the colt when he pulls back, charges ahead, or just plain jumps around. Initially, pony him on the right-hand side—away from the traffic—until he handles the traffic calmly. Make sure the horse you ride is good in traffic as it will influence the colt greatly. If the riding horse is steady and calm, the colt will take his cues from it and grow up to be safe and steady in traffic. This is a "must" because of today's heavy traffic and the few traffic-free roads left to drive on.

Ponying gives the colt a new "playground" and a look at more of his new world. He learns not to be afraid of things like mail boxes, fruit stands, bridges, running dogs, puddles of water, bicycles, and the hundreds of everyday hazards that the quiet riding horse takes for granted. He learns to move out at various gaits, to stop and stand, and to be mannerly beside other horses.

Once the colt shows no fear of traffic, he should be switched to the left side, where he does not have the quiet horse between him and the traffic. He will still gain reassurance from his companion as he becomes accustomed to cars and trucks.

The colt can also be ponyed from a cart, requiring a second person to hold the lead shank. This is great training for him as he learns right from the source what the cart looks and sounds like. Be very careful when ponying from a cart that the colt doesn't step into the spokes of the wheels. This can happen easily if the colt spooks at something and jumps sideways. The person with the lead shank must be very alert and watch the colt all the time.

Introduction of Harness

First, introduce the backpad and bellyband. Put this on in the horse's stall or with the horse on cross ties if he is accustomed to standing there to be groomed or handled. Familiar surroundings will be reassuring. The strange new harness should be the only new experience. Buckle the surcingle (bellyband) gradually but firmly and make it snug enough to prevent it slipping in any direction. If the colt shows no resistance or real fright, progress immediately to the training area on the lunge line. If the colt does react violently to the backpad, let him wear it in his stall for a time until he accepts it and settles down. Lunge him both ways of the circle until he has relaxed completely and pays no more attention to the harness, at both walk and trot. Next put on the crupper and buckle it in position. This could provoke a kicking spree if not done gently and in the proper order. Horses sometimes object strenuously and react violently to the addition of the crupper, especially if it is put on in an awkward or rough manner. However, if done with common sense and direction, all unpleasantness can be avoided.

First, unbuckle the bellyband and slide the backpad back to rest on the colt's loins. Let the crupper strap and crupper hang down on top of the horse's tail, reach through the crupper and grasp the tail with the right hand, and pull it through the crupper. With the left hand, slide the crupper up the tail to the dock, while the right hand cups and supports the tail from underneath— about eight inches back from the dock. Straighten out all the short tail hairs at the top of the tail with the left hand so they won't be jammed there and cause irritation. Grasp the crupper strap about halfway between the backpad and crupper and hold it firmly in place as the right hand GRADUALLY lowers the tail onto the crupper. This is the critical stage, just as the horse feels this foreign object on the sensitive underside of his tail. As you lower the tail, reassure the colt with your voice and be prepared to stop lowering if he becomes upset, then continue as he calms down. Do not let go until the tail is completely down and make sure the left hand retains the firm grasp of the crupper strap so that the crupper is not moving under his tail. If you were to drop the tail onto the crupper the first time, the colt could become very frightened, clamp his tail and rush forward. The harness would eventually slip down and fall off, entangling him in it. You would have a very "crupper-shy" colt for some time. A little extra time and gentleness at this stage is well worth the effort and will result in a quiet confident colt. If you have followed the exercises outlined in "Preparing the Green Colt for Driving" in Chapter 3, you should have little difficulty with the crupper.

Now, bring the backpad up into position on his back behind the withers and do up the bellyband. Adjust the length of the crupper strap so that the crupper is hanging below the dock about one-half inch. Next, go to the lungeing circle and work the colt as before both ways of the ring. Do not progress to the trot until he relaxes his tail on the crupper and stops worrying about it. After the colt has made a couple of rounds of the circle at the walk, it is advisable to halt him and check the adjustment of the crupper and strap. It more than likely has become loose, allowing the backpad to move forward up onto the withers. This is caused by the colt letting go with his tail or unclamping it from the crupper and, when he does, everything moves forward. So readjust the length of the crupper strap before continuing with the lesson. When the colt moves forward, his tail automatically lifts off the crupper, so you should have about an inch clearance between his tail and the crupper. If you allow any more than this, the crupper strap will flop from side to side on his croup and look very untidy; the crupper will no longer serve its purpose which is to hold the backpad in place. On the other hand, you must not have the crupper too tight as it will cause great irritation by constantly rubbing and will eventually scald the horse. This leads to other problems besides the obvious one—making the horse afraid of his crupper. Again, first impressions are the lasting ones; therefore, it is imperative that the colt's initial impression of the crupper is a positive one. When the colt is lungeing freely both ways of the ring at the walk and trot it is time to terminate this lesson and remove the harness. These first lessons should be short and should end on a happy note, i.e. the colt has done everything asked of him, understands his lesson, and has not been tired or hurt in any way.

To remove the harness, unbuckle the bellyband, and, holding the crupper strap firmly in position with the right hand, slide the backpad back onto the colt's loins. Change hands and hold the crupper strap with your left hand, lift the tail with your right and slowly slide the crupper down the tail until it passes the end of the tail bone, then pull it towards you and lift off the backpad and crupper simultaneously. You will notice that this process is the exact reverse of harnessing the colt described earlier. Walk the colt around for a few moments to cool him out, then brush out the harness marks and put him away with some feed as a reward. These small things are both noticed and appreciated by the colt.

Begin the next lesson exactly as before by putting on the backpad and crupper and lungeing the colt both ways of the ring to refresh his memory and warm him up. Now add an open bridle over his halter to which is still attached the lunge line. In our training program we ALWAYS wear a halter under the bridle. Never attach a lunge line to a bridle. Your colt is already accustomed to wearing a bit in his mouth so this does not cause him any problems. With bridle, backpad, and crupper on, lunge the colt both ways of the ring with frequent halts on the verbal command WHOA. The colt must learn to stand quietly with his harness on for long periods of time later on and now is the time to begin this habit. Next, put on the breastcollar and tie the traces up through the shaft loops to keep them from dangling and getting wound around the colt's legs. This part of the harness seldom causes any reaction on the colt's part, and you can continue to lunge him with his now-almost-complete harness on for another lesson or two.

How to Hold the Reins

The correct method of holding the reins for show driving also happens to be the easiest way, so I recommend the use of this method in all your lessons. By the time your colt has reached the stage of driving in a cart this method will have become a natural and comfortable habit.

The position of the reins in your hands must give you control, ease of lengthening or shortening your grip, maximum purchase and, last but far from least, project neatness and eye appeal. Reins can be straggling, unsightly pieces of leather when held improperly, and they are a potential hazard if the ends are allowed to dangle down around the spokes. It is an untidy sight to have the ends of a pair of reins dragging on the ground under a cart.

Grasp the reins, one in each hand, between the first and second fingers, with the rein running on through the hand between the palm and the fingers. Press down with the thumbs. Always remember to keep your thumbs down when driving, for both a better grip and sightliness. The bight of the left rein (the part below your hand) should be held between the third and little finger of the right hand. Pick this bight up by reaching over from right to left, grasping the left rein just below the hand between the third and last finger of the right hand and sliding the right hand along until the required loop is obtained.

To lengthen your grip, just slide back on the reins and readjust the bight accordingly. To shorten your grip, transfer the left rein to the right hand over the index finger where it is gripped by the thumb and palm. Now insert your left second finger between these reins, slide up the required amount and grip both reins firmly. Release the reins from the right hand and with it pick up the right rein immediately in front of the left hand. The left rein is already in the proper position between first and second fingers and so is the right because you've picked it up that way. Now you have shortened your reins with perfect control, i.e. all the time you were doing the maneuver, one or the other hand had complete control. Shortening the reins is often the moment when a driver loses control because he neglects to maintain a safe and positive grip all the way through the maneuver. It is essential to maintain constant and steady contact on BOTH reins throughout this transaction. One rein must not be allowed to flop loosely while you are changing your grip as this will cause the horse to veer the other way. You may then grab frantically for the other rein and jerk him badly in the process. This can develop into a habit whereby the horse always speeds up or veers out when he feels you beginning to change your grip on the reins. With practice, shortening the grip while driving will become an unconscious gesture, and if you are alert all the time, no large distances are involved in the move up the reins. You will be constantly shifting your grip to allow for variations in speed, terrain, and external conditions.

We always drive with two hands on the reins in the show ring in this country. When pleasure driving on quiet country roads or trails, it is often safe and restful to drive

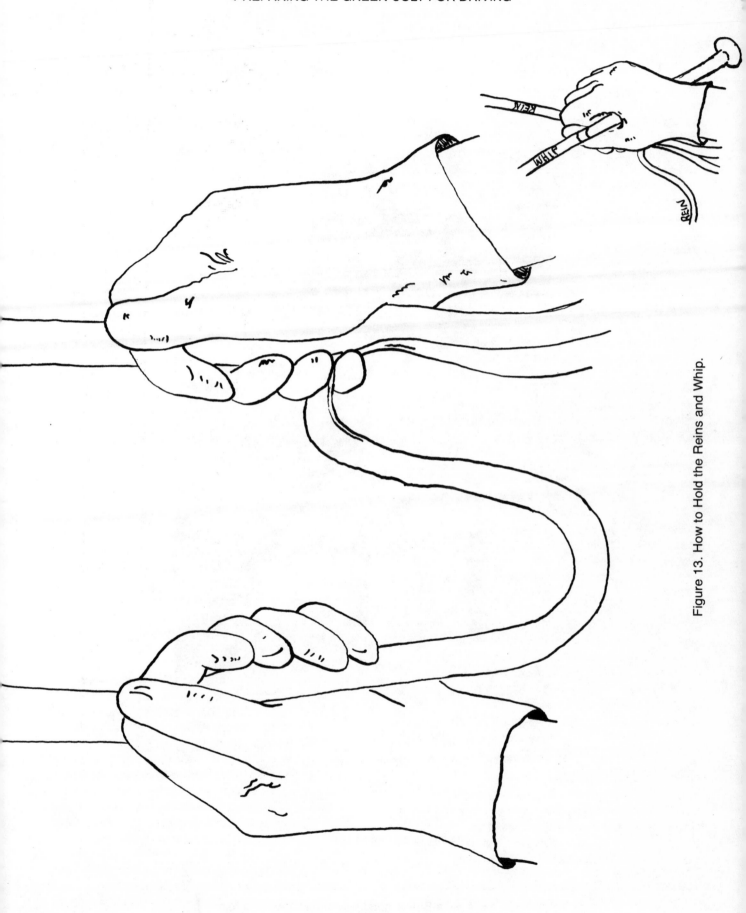

Figure 13. How to Hold the Reins and Whip.

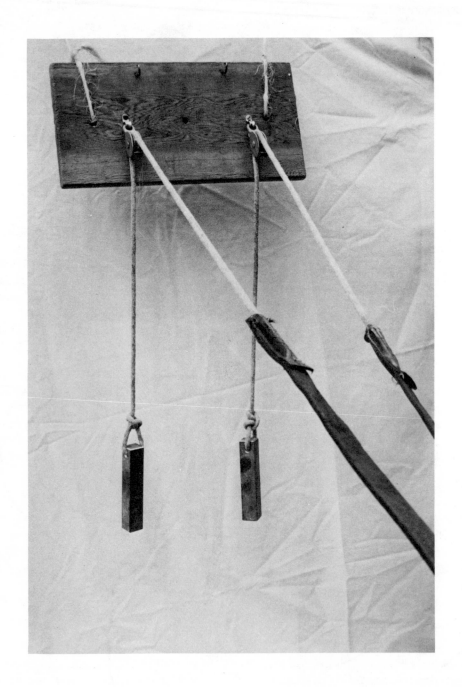

Figure 14. A Rein Board, complete with pulleys and reins.

with both reins in the left hand for periods of straight stretches, but when meeting cars or negotiating difficult country, two hands on the reins should be employed. The state of the horse's training is always a big consideration, as well as his steadiness. If he is a wanderer, there is no way you can steer him pleasureably with one hand.

Use the methods outlined above from the first lesson of "Ground Driving" on, and by the time the colt is driving in the cart you will pick up and hold the reins and whip properly without any effort or conscious thought on the matter.

Use of a Rein Board

Daily practice on a Rein Board is a rewarding exercise for the beginner driver. The Rein Board simulates actual driving in the safety of your barn or house without subjecting the horse to your learning fumbles and lack of experience. It is also a boon to more advanced drivers to perfect their technique and to practice in-hand driving with whip coordination.

The Rein Board consists of two rings or pulleys mounted on a board (or a wall) through which two reins with a weight at one end are threaded (see Figure 14). The weight should closely equal that of a normal horse being driven on the bit. I use pieces of lead weighing about one and three-quarter pounds. In a pinch, one or two horse shoes can be tied on the end as a substitute. The reins can be actual length leather reins, or sash cord from the weight back through the pulley—about six feet—then joined to a leather rein of about six feet. The latter arrangement is a bit more sophisticated and the rope runs more freely through the pulleys.

The driver stands back from the board, reins in proper driving position, with the weights about a foot off the ground. He practices picking up the reins, picking up the bight, steering right and left, halting, shortening and lengthening the reins, first without the whip and then, when fairly proficient, with the whip. He practices all these maneuvers to attain the ability to perform them with steady, fluid motions, *never* with jerks, and to get into the habit of shortening the reins from quick reflex action rather than conscious thought. The weights are a visual image of his prowess and actions. They show immediately whether or not the driver is smooth or jerky, whether the reins are even (MOST important) and whether or not you've just "lost" the horse as you turned. It improves your contact, teaches you to pull with the same force on *both* reins and gives you a greater insight into the reasons horses sometimes seem to misunderstand our commands.

One common problem beginners face is the fact that one hand is stronger than the other. If you are right handed, your right hand will usually, unbeknown to you, pull harder than the left. Often "crooked" horses are the result of this imbalance. Ridden horses have the same symptoms and problems. You MUST learn to pull evenly, and the use of a Rein Board is a great teaching aid as it allows you to see and correct right away such an occurrence.

Gloves

Gloves should always be worn when driving a horse. Buy gloves that are one-half to three-quarters of an inch longer than your fingers; within a short time they will have worked back into the shape of your hands. The fit of driving gloves is most important since it is impossible to drive properly in tight-fitting gloves. They should be of a soft, pliable, and strong type of leather (doeskin or goat leather, for example) and must be kept in clean and supple condition. Leather gloves reduce the chance of hands slipping on the reins, thus giving a stronger and steadier grip. They also give protection against the reins cutting into the hands. Many a horse that would be almost uncontrollable with bare hands after a few minutes of hard pulling is more readily or comfortably restrained when the driver has on a suitable pair of gloves.

In wet weather, string gloves should always be carried as leather gloves become impossible once wet. String gloves do not slip and give a good grip when wet. In cold wet weather, unless your horse is a puller, woolen gloves are best. Woolen gloves are warmer, even when wet, than either string or leather, but they tend to slip badly on the reins.

Start wearing gloves right away in the training of your colt and soon they will feel natural and comfortable. Before long, you will be pulling on your gloves before you pick up the reins as a matter of habit.

The Whip

Unless you are proficient in the use of a driving whip, it should not be carried during the early training of the colt. On the other hand, the whip is an extremely important factor in the art of driving. If you can persuade the owner of a well-trained and quiet horse to take you out for a few drives in his cart and let you practice with the whip, you will have a great advantage in the training of your colt. In addition to this, work with a Rein Board will be of great advantage. You can sit on a chair in a position simulating that of a cart and practice holding the reins and whip. Practice laying on the lash on an imaginary horse's side without losing contact on the reins. Practice turns, keeping the whip in position despite the movement of your hands. Make sure you are holding the reins and bight properly so you can become accustomed to the bulky feel of the whip held in the same hand as the bight. At first, they feel an impossible handful to manipulate, but you will be amazed how quickly you begin to feel comfortable. You can become downright handy with both reins and whip when practiced in this manner. A whip applied at just the right time and in just the right place achieves an instant effect and often a longer lasting one than any other method. The whip is as important to the good driver as are legs to a good rider. If a horse shies at an object, quick use of the whip on the opposite side can save the day as the horse's attention is diverted from the object that upset him. The whip is a means of keeping a horse "on the bit," as well as a means of punishment should the horse require it. Major Faudel-Phillips in his book "The Driving Book" says, "The whip is one of the most treasured possessions of a real coachman."

The driving whip is usually five and one-half feet long with a drop or lash of four to eight inches at the point. A slightly shorter whip with a longer lash is often just as effective and lighter to handle, but one must be very careful not to catch the longer lash in the spokes of a wheel. The whip should be held at the place it balances most comfortably, usually towards the top of the stock near the ferrule. Never hold a whip at the butt end; it is not a schoolroom pointer! The whip should be held in the right hand and carried at a FORTY-FIVE DEGREE AN-GLE both to the horse and to the ground, with the lash hanging vertically (see Figure 13). To use the whip as a mild reinforcement to the signal to move on faster, a circular movement of the right wrist lays the lash against the horse's side just behind the backpad. Except when punishing a horse severely, it is wise to use the whip on the sides of the horse only. Use of the whip on the back of the rear quarters can often initiate a kick.

A whip can also be thought of as a safety feature of driving. In a desperate situation, such as a runaway, the whip can be used to bring the horse under control much the same way as a sharp slap calms a hysterical person. The whip is often used as a means of distracting a horse's attention from frightening objects. With his mind on the whip (the greater of the two evils) the horse goes right by the frightening object—that is also called "horse psychology"! The ability to out-think your horse still remains your greatest advantage.

The whip should always be carried when driving for pleasure and is required in the show ring. It should be held in the hand at all times and not parked in the whip socket. If you need to use the whip, you usually need it instantly, and it is useless in the whip socket. Use the whip effectively but sparingly.

Chapter Four

Starting The Green Colt In Harness

Ground Driving

Attach the driving reins through the ring terrets on the backpad and buckle them onto the rings of the snaffle bit. First, begin driving the colt on the lungeing circle which he already knows well. He will follow with very little guidance. Walk beside his flank on the inside of the circle, about two feet out from his flank and back a foot or two to the rear. This position is extremely vital for obtaining utmost control for the various stages of training from now on. In this position, you have tremendous leverage, using the ring terret as a fulcrum, and are out of the way of the horse's heels should he act up. Make sure at this time that you have your driving gloves on and are holding the reins in the proper manner. Walking in this position, drive the colt around the circle and gradually apply more pressure on the outside rein to bring the colt into an ever-widening circle until he is using the whole ring. Now begin to guide the colt into wide turns, which at first will be awkward, hexagonal, and jerky, but none of these things matter at this stage. The important thing is to have the colt begin to respond to the pull of the rein and turn. As long as he turns, don't worry about anything else. Your hands must be fluid, relaxed, and gentle, yet firm and positive. One hand must give as much as the other takes, otherwise the colt cannot turn. Beginners often overlook this fact and wonder why the colt does not respond to the pull. Use body pull, not just arms and hands, to smoothen out the signals. If only hands and arms are used, the pull is too jerky and unpleasant for the colt. Often he will resist and throw his head or have other adverse reactions which could become a habit with continued provocation. *Hands* are extremely important.

The correct position of your arms when driving is important both from a standpoint of utmost control and sightliness. The reins should form a straight line from the ring terret to your elbow. Your forearm and hand become an extension of the rein, transmitting impulses with finesse and smoothness from your body. Any dip or change of this straight line results in loss of fluid contact and a jerk on the horse's mouth. When you pull on a rein, pull back towards your hip, keeping this straight line rather than raising or lowering your hands. This will maintain the firm but light contact and produce smoother driving maneuvers and happier horses. Be sure to keep your wrists loose and flexible and avoid tenseness. Tense, tight wrists make smooth, fluid driving contact impossible. You will find the Rein Board a great help to develop this form and suppleness.

Work both ways of the ring and very soon the colt will be responding easily and readily to the pressure on the rein and his turns will automatically begin to smoothen out. Always praise your colt when he does well. Frequent reassurances of "good boy" in a soothing and pleased tone create and maintain a quiet and happy atmosphere. Remember, too, to keep the lessons short and interesting.

Continue ground driving with the open bridle, making the lessons more difficult and asking more of your colt each day. When you reverse direction, on the diagonal, do smooth crossovers, adjusting your reins as you cross behind the colt. This requires quick footwork and even pressure on the reins all the way across, keeping the colt straight all the time. Your hands must function independently of your body—they must never bounce up, down, or sideways regardless of the motions the rest of your body is going through. Cornering is a prime area for mistakes. You must stay in close to your horse on the corners. The tendency is to walk a smaller curve than your horse on corners and this usually results in a colt spinning around towards you. Don't overwalk the colt on corners! Keep the proper, prescribed distance from the colt *all the way* around the corner, thus maintaining even and firm contact on both reins. Be ready always to apply more pressure on the *outside* rein to prevent the colt from falling-in or spinning on the corners. As your training progresses, you will find that the outside rein is the most important one in *all* maneuvers. The inside rein indicates a turn, but the outside rein dictates how far and stabilizes the direction.

Now do figure eights and serpentines making the colt bend slightly into his turns and begin ever so gradually to instigate turns on the haunches, making the colt cross his feet as he turns on the spot. You must have very steady hands for your ground work; the reins should never flop up and down or sideways. As you change direction in the ring, you must change the side from which you are driving; and as you change over, your hands must retain contact and control without jerking or dropping reins. When you do a figure eight, for instance, you must change sides right at the center of the "eight." When the colt is managing figure eights lengthwise in the whole ring, it is time to make them more difficult by doing them across the ring. Both you and the colt will have to think faster and turn much shorter while maintaining the proper smoothness and even loops on either end of the "eight." This will require more bending on the colt's part and your outside rein will keep him following the proper curvature. Do smaller circles as well, perhaps a 30-foot diameter circle. Make sure you do them in both directions so that the colt does not become one-sided. Put a marker in the ring and practice driving a circle around it, out about 12 to 15 feet, looking ONLY at the marker. You must start to feel the horse through the reins without looking at him. When you are driving in the show ring or out on the road, you must be able to watch all around you while maintaining a proper course with your horse, so start now to learn to drive by "braille"! You will eventually be able to feel his every movement through the reins.

A bonus fringe benefit derived from driving a horse in the position just described is the development of the driver's hands. His hands become very sensitive to the feel of the horse's mouth and learn to transmit continuous and infinitesimal messages through the reins. His hands and arms also become independent of his body movements and gain great steadiness and control which will be a decided advantage to him when he is riding as well as driving.

Halts

Figures, turns, and circles should be frequently interspersed with halts. A horse must learn to stand quietly for long periods of time in a buggy. Usually there is no room for him to fidget, jump, or fuss as there may be other horses, buggies, cars or spectators all around. There are times when your safety depends upon the horse's ability to stand still, so your training must include this lesson right from the start. At the beginning, ask only for short halts of ten or twenty seconds and, as the colt's training and concentration improve, ask for longer halts. Watch your colt carefully during these periods of standing, and when you see him preparing to move, quickly give the command to move forward. This way he will feel it was YOUR idea and he was obeying, not moving off on his own hook. Always make your halts in a different part of the ring, so that the colt does not come to associate the halt with any one spot. When he is standing at the halt, relax his reins so that there is no contact with his mouth; in other words, a reward. If he moves off unbidden, tell him WHOA with a slight pull on the reins (a punishment) and relax the reins again. He will soon associate the halt with the reward and prolong it willingly.

To accomplish these halts, say "Whoa" (in a meaningful tone of voice), then stop walking and let the colt come up into your hands (through the bit and reins). Don't pull or jerk on him, just set your hands firmly as you stop and the colt will halt squarely and with a good head position. As soon as he has come to a full stop, give with the reins to release his bit pressure—his reward—and praise him. Make him stand as long as is feasible at this stage of training, then take up light contact and cluck him on as you audibly tell him "walk on." With repeated practice, your colt will become accustomed to standing with a loose rein. This makes it a pleasure to drive him later out on roads.

Never drop or set your reins down unless you have a groom or helper at the horse's head—a runaway in harness with or without a buggy is one of the most frightening and disastrous of experiences that can happen.

Bitting Harness

Up until this point in the colt's training, you could just as easily have used a bitting harness. In fact, if you have a bitting harness, definitely use it instead of your good driving harness. It does all the things covered so far—with the exception of the breast-collar which is unimportant at this stage—and is far more durable and less prone to damage than a driving harness. Leave the side reins snapped onto the backpad when they are not in use (or take them off altogether) and adjust the side checks loosely enough so they do not hinder the horse's

Figure 15. A properly fitted Bitting Harness.

head carriage at all. Follow the same procedures given in the previous pages until the colt is driving happily and handily on the reins.

If you have a bitting harness, it can now be used in its own right and you can buckle on the side reins and adjust the side checks (see Figure 15). Adjust the side reins so that they just begin to flex the colt's head, making the outside rein about three inches longer than the inside one (when you change direction on the circle you will have to reverse this procedure). The side checks should be tightened until the colt's head is held up higher than he would normally hold it when at rest. The colt's head is now more or less fixed in a preset position — with considerable leeway at this stage — and as he is lunged on the circle he will learn to move with a steady head carriage and to give and flex to the feel of the side reins. Continue lungeing him with the full bitting rig and, gradually over a period of weeks, increase the tension of both side reins and side checks until he carries his head in the position you wish without resistance to the harness. Never leave the side reins and side checks on for more than 10 or 15 minutes at a time in these early stages of training; your colt has undeveloped neck and back muscles which could be strained. What we are trying to do is stretch the muscle that runs along the top of the colt's neck and to atrophy (get rid of) any strong build-up of muscle on the underside of his neck — from his throat to his chest. This can only be done gradually as muscles do not change overnight; thus, we must be careful not to overdo any of the sessions. We could not only hurt his neck but also sour him on the whole harness idea. He could begin to associate his pain with the harness. Naturally we want to avoid this situation. When in doubt about the tension of the side reins and check rein, always make them looser instead of tighter. For a change of pace and a rest, disconnect the side reins and drive the colt on the long driving reins for a few minutes. This prevents the colt from becoming bored or sour and holds his interest while continuing all aspects of his lessons. It also develops your colt's mind because he has to concentrate on progressively more difficult and diverse requests from his trainer.

Free lungeing with the bitting rig on is good for your colt. Make certain that you make the outside rein longer than the inside one to ensure that the colt bends with the circle. Change the gaits frequently, include *halts* and standing still. The colt's respect and obedience will grow and develop greatly from these free sessions. The free lungeing sessions are done in a closed round ring, not out in an open area.

Driving Bridle with Blinkers

The colt has now reached the stage where he must wear his driving bridle with blinkers. Put this bridle on and adjust it as explained in the chapter on "Adjustments," making the overdraw checkrein just tight enough to keep his head higher than its AT REST position (refer to Figure 8). Attach the driving reins to the bit, position yourself to the side and rear of his flank and have your helper lead off the colt for the first time. Horses' reactions to blinkers vary — some refuse to take a step with them on at first, some take fright and spin around, and some take no notice at all. Until you have tried them on your colt, you will have no way of knowing just what he will do. Therefore, have your helper lead the colt off from the front (as you drive him) to give him confidence and show him what you wish him to do, as well as to help control him should the necessity arise. Remember to stay in position near the flank, especially if he acts up and spins, or he may turn underneath the reins and you will have to let go to prevent both of you becoming tangled. Once the colt is moving more or less steadily the helper can disconnect the shank and step back. As the colt has already learned how to drive well on the reins and responds readily to his bit, it is only a matter of accustoming him to the blinkers and the fact that his vision is now restricted. From now on he must have absolute confidence in his driver and respond to his directions even though he cannot see everything around him or what is making noises out of sight behind his blinkers. Through the use and acceptance of these blinkers, he will develop a respect for his driver which will eventually grow to such an extent that the driver can ask him to go through or into the most frightening places and have him obey despite his natural fear. Conditioning is a wonderful asset; keep in mind that you are working on this asset every time you give your colt a lesson. Bad habits are also a product of conditioning, but of the wrong kind!

At this time, add the running martingale to the colt's harness. It should be adjusted so that when you are driving with the colt's head in a normal position it does not restrict the rein at all. It immediately exerts a downward pressure on the reins if the colt throws his head up. This downward pressure has the effect of settling a bit on the bars of the mouth and thus giving you the full and proper use of the bit. The rein should be a straight line from the bit to the rein terret. The martingale is a safety factor as well as a training aid. If a horse throws up his head suddenly, preparatory to taking off, the martingale is a self-correcting, self-punishing instrument. It applies itself instantly, far faster than our own actions could ever achieve. Self punishment — cause and effect — is a far better teacher than our chastisement. A horse remembers a hurt like that and tries to avoid a repetition. A running martingale is of tremendous value in the training of horses, and as some

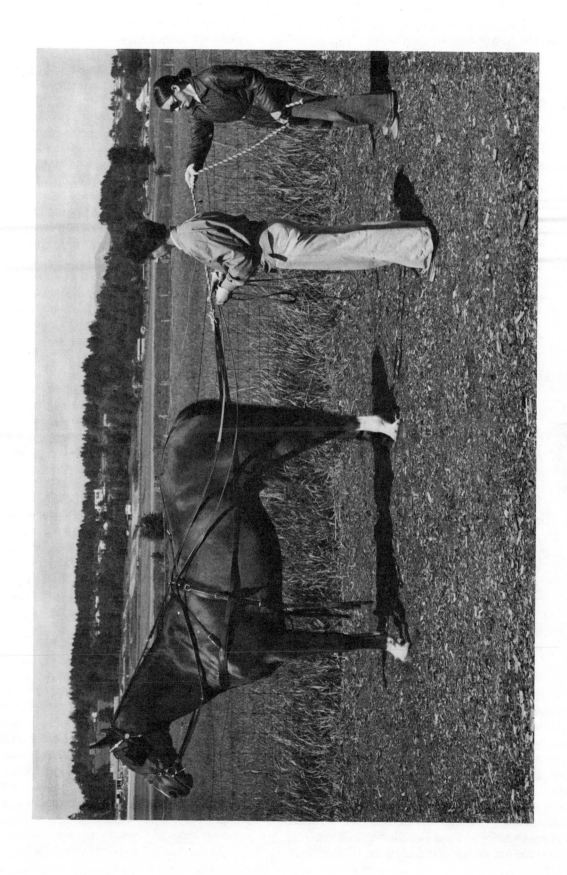

Figure 16. Use of Trace Aids as a Training Aid.

breeds are required to show with them, it is a good practice to use one from now on in your training.

With the driving bridle and martingale on, repeat all the previous lessons until your colt is doing turns, figures, halts, and circles readily, smoothly, and with steady control.

Use of Traces as a Training Aid

The transition from plain ground driving to pulling a load, hemmed in by shafts can be a frightening and difficult step for a colt to understand and cope with. To lessen this trauma and to prepare him gradually for the job, it is wise to introduce another step or phase in our colt's training. This step is called "trace aids" and teaches the colt how to pull a load and to understand and enjoy the new requirement. This step takes only a few minutes' time but is invaluable in establishing one of the most important functions of a horse—that of pulling.

With the breastcollar in its proper position, untie the traces, run them through the shaft loops (to give them some vertical support), then tie the ends together with a piece of baler twine or strong shoelace. Tie them with a bow or knot that you can easily undo later. Attach a lead rope, about six feet, to the twine via the snap on its end. Have your helper hold this line, supporting the traces upwards, and walk about five or six feet behind the colt, i.e. out of reach of his heels, as you drive the colt from your normal position at the side (see Figure 16). Follow the large track to give the longest straight stretches for the first part of this lesson. Have your helper gradually put some contact on the traces by pulling to the rear, then release them for a few seconds and repeat. Always release upwards, to keep the rope and traces well away from the colt's hocks. This gives the colt his first experience with pulling and he will likely hesitate or try to stop—keep him going! He must never get the idea that he can evade pulling or even think of evading it. A balky horse is usually the result of evasion—an evasion he got away with. So you must keep him moving, and if a strong cluck does not get immediate results, slap him on the flank with the rein or whip. Have your helper put more and more pull on the traces for very short bursts—10 to 15 feet—with complete releases in between to relax and reward the colt. These pulls should be very gradually increased and must be smooth and steady; try not to jerk on the colt's chest. When the colt relaxes and lowers his head into a position that allows him to use his pulling muscles properly, he will become much steadier. After a few minutes, the colt will usually learn to push his chest into the breastcollar and pull steadily and willingly. This lesson should not exceed 15 minutes, for it is strenuous

both mentally and physically for your colt and you do not want him to develop a sore muscle at this early stage and get the wrong impression of driving. When he pulls readily and easily on the large track, have the helper begin to swing out from side to side on the traces, gently at first and to one side only. The colt will be excited at this new movement and perhaps a bit sensitive to the trace which is now rubbing his opposite flank. Again, do not let him stop! Keep him going, and try to keep him straight. His quarter will fall inwards with the pull of the traces for he has no balance as yet, and his head will turn outwards to offset the quarters. He MUST BE KEPT STRAIGHT. Have the helper keep swinging back and forth to this side from the rear, still exerting just a medium pull on the traces until the colt can keep his balance and pull straight forward. Now change direction and do the same thing to the other side. When the colt can keep his balance and pull straight, have the helper swing right over from side to side without stopping in the middle as before, and put more and more pull on the traces until the colt is having to work at it to keep going. He has now learned to pull!

Practice halting and have the colt start off with a pull on his chest (just a slight pressure at first to encourage him to go forwards) and work up to him being able to start off under fairly strong pressure. The feel of the traces on his flanks also prepares the colt for the feel of the poles which will touch him in the same place and they come as much less of a shock to him after this step is perfected. Just prior to ending his lesson, the helper should rub the traces up and down the horse's flank, gaskins, hocks and lower legs—still standing well back at the end of the lead rope. This up-and-down, then flopping action of the traces will accustom him to their feel. Later on when some piece of leather does come loose and touch him back there, he will not panic or be surprised.

Breeching

If it is your intention to use breeching on your horse, now is the proper time to introduce it. Run the loin strap through the crupper strap where the slot is provided and adjust it so that the breeching seat lies on the flat part of his buttock. Buckle the breeching straps snugly to the shaft loops and ground drive the colt through the figures and circles he has been doing. With the breeching buckled tightly in this manner, pressure is put on his quarters to simulate the pressure he will feel when the breeching is used in actual work to stop the load. You need not spend much time on this stage unless the colt objects to the breeching, in which case the lesson must continue until he accepts it and carries on quietly.

Chapter Five

Work In Poles

Completion of the previous chapter's work constitutes the preparation of your colt for work in poles. When a horse is ground driving well, doing smooth figures, circles and turns, showing attention and obedience to your commands, and pulling steadily and balanced in the traces, he must be considered ready for this next step.

Poles — Design and Construction

Poles are simply two long, slim trees joined together in a wedge shape, very similar at first glance to the old Indian travois design. The poles should be cut green just before you intend to use them. At this stage they will be resilient; they will GIVE rather than break should a horse fall, lie down, or jam them against a solid object. It is very important that a horse never learn that he CAN break anything. A horse that has no respect for his equipment (or his trainer) is a potentially dangerous animal and this is an extremely difficult attitude to cure. Old dry poles should *never* be used. They will break instantly and easily with an impact and usually break with a long sharp shard or point sticking out. A horse can be badly injured by these dangerous poles; the sharp point can go right through him under certain conditions. Your lessons must always be given in a manner that teaches the horse respect for any equipment used on or with him. With this in mind, you must use equipment that is sound and methods that minimize any chance of breakage — thus, the use of green poles at this critical stage of training. The type of wood used will depend on what kind of trees grow in your vicinity and is immaterial, although a soft wood is preferable to a hard wood. In areas where trees are scarce or laws prohibit cutting trees, an alternative that works very well is poles constructed of black ABS pipe. Use a piece of two-inch ABS pipe, 10 feet long, joined by a joiner patch to a one-foot piece of one and one-half inch ABS pipe. This allows the shaft loops to slide on easily and provides a "stop" for them. For the crossbar, use a light piece of one-half inch plywood about eight inches wide. A two-inch wooden dowel inserted inside the 10-foot length of pipe will provide better rigidity and performance.

The poles should be three inches in diameter at the ends (back end) and as straight as possible. Whittle or chip the front ends down to a size that will slide easily into the shaft loops. The length can be from 10 to 12 feet, but no longer than 12 feet or they become too cumbersome for both horse and trainer to handle. The poles should be considerably thicker at the back ends to add the stability and weight which is needed for effective work in poles. I prefer to use 11-foot poles for horses and 9-foot poles for ponies.

Lay the two poles on the ground in a wedge shape, with the tips about 22 inches apart and splayed out wider towards the rear (see Figure 17). Measure 6 foot 3 inches back from the tips and bolt on a 2 × 6 inch plank across the poles, which should be about 48 inches at this spot. Screw in an eye screw on either side of this plank — these will be used to attach the traces and will, in effect, be pulling the whole weight of the poles so they must be strong. Taper the front 18 inches of the poles to ensure an easy and smooth entry into the shaft loops. When you put your colt into the poles for the first time you don't want to be held up for minutes trying to JAM oversize tips into the shaft loops. Nor do you want the poles to fit so tightly that you can't get them out in a hurry. Make sure the poles are smooth where the horse will rub against them, i.e. back to the crossbar. You will usually have to remove several knots and sharp bits of bark. You want to be certain that your colt's actions are because of the poles themselves and not due to something jabbing or bothering him. It is important that the crossbar be placed about six feet back from the tips rather than at the back end. At the six-foot position it simulates the actual crossbar on the buggy shafts as well as adding rigidity and stability to the poles. It also makes the poles better balanced and easier to pull and turn. There are good reasons for the designated length of the poles. Using this length, the part immediately in front of the crossbar will touch the horse's flank in approximately the same place as will the shafts on the cart or buggy. Also, the poles will be high enough at this point to prevent the colt from getting a leg over the pole if he jumps around or acts up. If the poles are shorter than 10 feet, they will be too low at the flank and will be a potential hazard on every turn, even with a quiet horse.

Introduction of Poles

With the newly constructed poles lying in the center of the ring, bring in the colt with his harness on and drive him around as usual. Bring him up to the poles and let him assure himself that they are harmless, then continue driving him in figures and circles with an occasional pass beside and eventually over the poles. Soon the colt will be paying no attention to them and will have accepted them as part of the ring scenery. Now have your helper stand between the tips of the poles and raise them up. The colt will notice the difference and must be taken up to them again and reassured as to their nature. Next, have your helper drag the poles slowly AWAY from the colt as you encourage him to follow along behind. Once he recovers from his initial surprise and responds to your commands on the reins, drive him up past the poles, circle them, and take turns with your helper in passing each other. When the colt begins to adjust to the new situation, urge him to go closer (up till now you have likely been giving them a wide berth) and make sure you accustom him to seeing the poles on either side. What he accepts on one side always is a new experience when seen on the other side. Continue this "playing tag" with the poles until the colt goes quietly and has accepted them completely. He will now have a mental picture of them, and, even though they are out of sight, will not be frightened as he has "catalogued" them and knows without seeing them exactly what they are. He is learning to "see" the sound. As stated before, a horse learns by repetition and habit, and the purpose of the above exercise is to ingrain the sight and sound of the poles into his memory.

Give the colt one good lesson in this manner before hitching him. Give more if he is still apprehensive of them.

Hitching the Colt in Poles

Position the poles at the top end of one of the long sides of the ring. The purpose of this is to allow the longest straight stretch possible before you have to turn. You want the colt to accustom himself to the pull and sound of the poles before they touch him so that he has the minimum of new sensations at any one time. It is on turns that a horse is most apt to become excited, so try to make them as easy for him as possible.

Attach a safety line to the colt's halter under the driving bridle and have your helper stand at his head. Another assistant would be useful if available but is not absolutely necessary. Position the colt directly in front of the poles and as close to them as possible. Have the helper stand in front of him in control with the safety line. Bring the poles up over the top of the colt's croup, then down and through the shaft loops (this is where a second assistant comes in handy to do the second side). Never draw the shafts straight up towards the colt's flank where they will poke him if he moves sideways at all. Horses become quite shy of shafts for this reason and it is both uncomfortable and unnecessary. Untie the traces and bring them back onto the hooks on the crossbar, next to the horse, not outside the poles. The traces must be adjusted so that the tips of the shafts do NOT extend beyond the point of the colt's shoulder; if they do, the shafts will poke him in the neck every time he turns and soon he will make all his turns with his head tilted outwards to avoid being jabbed—a very bad habit. Adjust the shaft loops so the shafts at this point are down about 12 inches from his back; the poles are easier to pull and safer if they are fairly high. Do not buckle or wrap the wrap straps around the poles. If it becomes necessary to get the colt out of the poles in a hurry, we want a minimum of straps to be undone. The wrap straps are unnecessary in poles anyway. Either let them hang down in loops, or thread the billet end through the shaft loop and let it hang loosely.

Check and adjust your reins, making sure you have the bight up out of the way so you don't trip on it. Take up position beside the horse exactly as you did when ground driving—out from the flank and back a pace (see Figure 18). If you get in too close to your horse, you will get hit by the poles which splay out behind. Be careful to keep the proper position, especially in the turns, so as to have the most control and ease of handling. NEVER walk between the poles when driving! You have

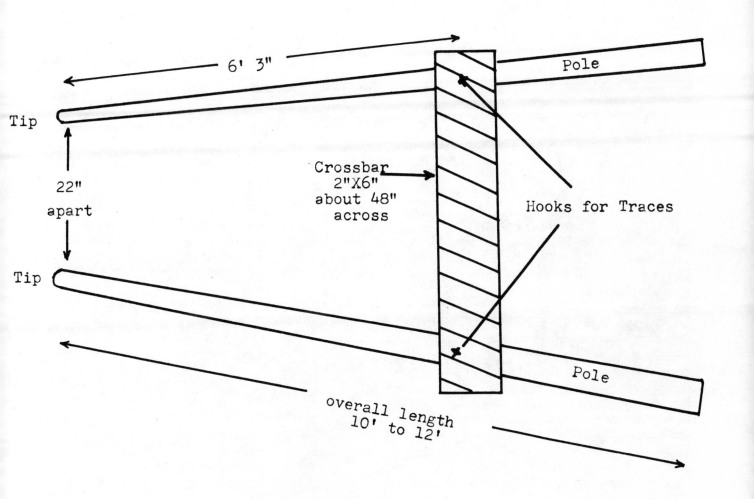

Figure 17. Construction of Poles

Figure 18. Driving in Poles

the least control when directly behind your horse, and if he acts up at all you are likely to get badly hurt as you will be trapped in between flailing poles. The only time it is permissible to step between the poles is when you are changing sides in the center of a figure eight, and then it is done as a crossing-over motion which is completely different from walking between them. Always drive from the inside of the direction in which you are going: for instance, when going to the left you should be on the left side of the poles.

Take up light contact on your reins and have your helper lead off the colt. The colt will be able to see him and, gaining confidence, will go more quietly and readily. Continue straight down the side of the ring and start your turn BEFORE you get too far into it, to avoid jamming the colt in it the first time. It is very important that the colt does not get upset on this first turn; if you go too deeply into the turn, the colt will get sideways in the shafts trying to turn them sharply. The feel of the poles simultaneously on the near shoulder and the off flank can be quite alarming to him. The first few turns should be as large and smooth as possible. If done smoothly, the poles will barely touch the colt's shoulder and will not touch his flank at all, thus accustoming him to one thing at a time. Although your helper is in front and leading the colt forward, you should be using the reins as a steering and guiding control; the helper is really only a safety feature and a confidence symbol—YOU are the driver! At the corner, if the colt does not respond readily to your signal on the reins, tell your helper to bring him around gradually with the lead rope (the colt must not be jerked into hitting the poles with his shoulder) and use this assistance on the turns as long as necessary. The colt has to learn how to maneuver these poles around a corner. They offer considerable resistance due to their length and rigidity and the colt has to be taught to push and lean inwards to accomplish a turn (eventually by crossing his legs). Until he has learned this, he will likely need assistance on the initial part of a turn. If you are attentive and steady, the poles should never hit the colt on a turn; rather, they will touch him gently and retain this soft contact the whole way around. This can only be accomplished by utilizing the great sensitivity to be found in your hands. They must be constantly "giving" and "taking" with slight squeezes of pressure on the reins to accomplish these smooth turns. Again, your Rein Board will be of great assistance in achieving this light, quick response. Your reflexes must be faster than those of the horse to correct his movements the instant they are begun. If they are not, the path of the horse will be jerky and erratic, and you will run the risk of having a frightened colt career off first one pole then the other.

As the next movement with your colt involves a crossover, these should be practiced first on the wall. Set the poles up against the wall or fence at the same height as if they were on the horse. Connect a pair of driving reins to the top board in the center of the poles and practice sliding down, crossing over, and then sliding back up the reins to the first position. When you can acccomplish this maneuver with ease and without losing control, you are ready to try it with your colt in the poles.

Unless the colt is acting badly, after the second or third corner your helper should gradually move back behind the colt's blinkers—out of sight as far as the colt is concerned but retaining the safety line which should be slack. Otherwise, the helper could become a crutch to the colt. From now on, this line is strictly a safety line, and the colt should take all commands and control from the driver with the reins. But until the colt is completely under your control, continue to have the safety line on and the helper walking quietly out of his sight. Gradually make the turns a bit smaller so that the colt is having to shove the poles around more forcibly and at the same time becoming accustomed to the feel of them on shoulder and flank. Make sure you do an equal amount of work each direction of the ring to prevent the colt from becoming one-sided, an all-too-common fault. When you reverse the ring, you must change sides and this maneuver can be rather tricky. Always do the first few reverses on the long diagonal of the ring, i.e. after crossing the end of the ring, go diagonally across the ring heading for the opposite end. This gives you the furthest distance in which to accomplish the reverse and allows the turns to be large and easy. In reversing the ring, you should change sides right at the middle of the straight part of the diagonal. To do this, slide down the reins far enough to permit you to step over the two poles easily where they are fairly low, then slide back up the reins to the proper position. While sliding down the reins and stepping over the poles, you must retain firm and steady control of the colt's mouth. You must keep him STRAIGHT as you do the crossover. This exercise, mastered easily with practice, is of tremendous value in your campaign to make your hands independent of body movements. When sliding back up the reins, be careful to hold both reins in one hand, keeping the same contact with the mouth, while the other hand takes up position further up the reins. The proper way to hold the reins has been covered in a previous chapter and if held in this manner the problem of moving up or down them is greatly simplified. Actually, you can be flexible in the method used; it is the results that count. As long as the colt continues on quietly and in the direction required, the gymnastics involved in changing sides can be tailored to individual abilities.

For the first lesson in the poles, it is best to stop around the 15-minute mark. You can overdo it at this stage, for it is always a temptation to carry on longer just to see how much the colt can do. Whether he shows it or not, this lesson has been a mental strain for the colt, and to tire him mentally is as detrimental to your training program as to wear him out physically. If he is going quietly both ways of the ring, turning nice smooth large corners, be satisfied with 15 minutes of work. However, if he is fighting the poles, moving jerkily and having to be lead and restrained by the safety line constantly, continue the lesson until he settles to the point stated above. If after 25–30 minutes he is still upset, unhitch him and go back to more ground driving and orientation as this is obviously the problem.

Pat him, make a fuss over him, and let him know how pleased you are with his performance if the lesson has gone well. Horses are sensitive to praise and should always be praised when they have done well; it makes a real contrast then when you scold them for doing wrong and they soon learn to try for praise.

Be careful taking the colt out of the poles. Halt him and have the helper stand at his head while you undo the traces and tie them up. Slide the shaft loops off and have the helper lead the colt straight forward as you support the poles.

Start the next lesson the same way as the previous one, i.e. have the helper drag the poles around first to refresh the colt's memory and drive some figure eights and circles to warm up the colt before hitching him in the poles. Hitch him in the same fashion and the same place as before and again have the helper lead him off the first time. This time, however, the helper ought to be able to drop back after the first corner and continue as safety man. Do the same things as before—turn large smooth corners, reverse the ring and work from the other side. Continue driving large smooth corners with frequent figure eights and halts, and gradually tighten up the corners until you can make a smooth circle using only half the ring. This is still a large circle, but involves constant and steady turning on the colt's part and practically forces him to cross his legs to accomplish. Take care that you nudge the inside rein frequently to achieve an inward bend to the colt's head. He must look *into* the turns and his body must bend according to the arc of the turn. Practice smaller figure eights across the ring, smaller circles and serpentines. Make sure you do each new figure both ways of the ring. To do circles, pick a landmark in the ring and look *only* at that point as you drive your colt around it. You must learn to drive by feel.

You cannot always look constantly at your horse; you must be able to look around at the changing scenery and know exactly—by feel alone—what your horse is doing.

Set up patterns of cones (markers) and practice driving exact figures around and through them. In this manner, you and your colt will become more adept and it will keep the colt from becoming bored.

It is time now to progress further with the turns on the haunches. The colt has the background and ability now to accomplish this maneuver and requires only careful guidance to bring it off. Halt him on the track, going to the left, as you ask him to walk on signal with your left rein. As he moves forward, bring him around to the left about 45 degrees and then go forward briskly before you lose the momentum. As you try this turn, always be prepared for the colt to stall if the turn is sharper than he expects, and MAKE HIM MOVE FORWARD. Never let him reach a full stop because this can become an evasion and a bad habit later on. Make the turn only as tight as he can do reasonably well and, as time goes by, he will be able to do 90 degrees easily. Drive the colt in fairly small figure eights and circles with several halts. The halts should be prolonged more and more until the colt will stand quietly for a minute or two without fidgeting or becoming excited. The poles help to teach a colt not to try to back up as an evasion—he cannot move backwards easily as the ends of the poles dig in! Thus, early on, the colt learns the futility of this move; later on, your cart may be saved from a disastrous end because of this lesson. A cart WILL go backwards, and, once started running backwards in a cart, a colt will continue until something gives, and that something is usually the cart as it goes through a fence. A colt should NEVER be asked or taught to back up until he has learned to *go forward properly.* I usually drive a colt in the cart for two to three months before asking him to back up, then I teach him first from the ground without the cart.

If possible, do some work on a gravel surface with the poles. The poles make a terrible noise on gravel and help prepare the colt for the many noises he will hear when driving on the road or in the show ring. First, have your helper drag the poles on the gravel as you ground drive the colt behind to let him see what is making the noise; then hitch him and keep the safety line on as you drive him on the gravel. If you have done the preparatory work in poles well, the noise from the gravel should not cause undue excitement. The colt will likely be a bit tense at first and may spook a few times, but will probably settle down easily and not pay any attention to the noise within a few minutes. Do not prolong this lesson; as soon as he is going quietly go back into the ring with the poles.

The length of time necessary for a colt to spend in poles varies with his temperament and disposition. A week of daily lessons is often adequate for a quiet and easy-going colt, while a high-spirited and nervous type may need two or more weeks. Time is not the criterion; again, it is the results that count, but I consider one week the necessary and also the minimum time spent at this stage. When the colt drives in poles steadily, performing circles and figures, when he halts and stands quietly, when he does turns on the haunches smoothly and willingly, he is ready to move on to the next stage of training—hitching in the cart.

Chapter Six

Hitching In The Cart

Type of Cart

Now the colt is ready to be hitched to a vehicle. It is preferable to hitch him to a two-wheeled cart first. This is very similar to the poles to which he has become accustomed and it will not jacknife and upset as will a four-wheeled buggy when turned too short. A cart is far more rugged and less breakable than a buggy and usually less expensive. A good type of cart for training and all-around use is the Cross-Country cart with wooden spokes in the wheels, hard rubber tires and nearly all-wood construction (see Figure 19). This old-fashioned type of cart with wheels about three to four feet in diameter, gives the smoothest ride over rough ground and is virtually unbreakable. The cart should be well-sprung to provide comfort for both horse and driver, and must be well balanced to eliminate any excess force on the horse's back. There must be NO upward pull on the bellyband (overbalanced to the rear) nor extreme downward push on the backpad (overbalanced to the front). The cart is in balance when there is just sufficient weight on the shafts to keep them in their resting place in the shaft loops. Other popular types of cart are the light metal style or wooden jogging cart with wire spokes and pneumatic tires. These carts are often of metal construction, very lightweight and excellent for some purposes, but they are extremely vulnerable and breakable, sometimes producing upsetting metallic rattles, and cannot be used to advantage on rough terrain. If it is your intention to use the cart solely as a training vehicle in the ring, this type of cart will serve the purpose very nicely. I personally prefer a heavier cart even for training, as the extra weight teaches the colt to pull properly and builds up his muscles. I have confidence, too, that this sturdy cart will withstand severe punishment should the colt act up violently. If a cart cannot be found of either type mentioned above, a very useful and inexpensive cart can be made up using a car axle and steel tubing. An axle of the type found on small cars with two car wheels provides an excellent base on which to build a seat of some sort, and shafts can be made from steel tubing bent in the manner of buggy shafts. Care must be taken to ensure that this cart is well-balanced because its heavier construction could cause severe strain to the colt. However, you should use the type of cart you can locate most easily and the type will not change the driving methods you use. If the vehicle is really heavy, collar and hames style of harness will work best. If such is unavailable, use an extra-wide, well-padded breastcollar to spread the force over a larger area, making it easier on the horse.

Familiarization

Prepare the colt for the cart in the same manner you used for the poles. Park the cart in the middle of the ring, bring in the colt and let him smell it and look at it from all angles. Lift the shafts and drop them a few times to let him hear the ensuing noise and assure himself that it is harmless. Drive the colt around the ring next, with full harness on, passing close by the cart each time until he no longer pays any attention to it. A good idea is to have the cart parked nearby all the time you are working in poles so that the colt will be familiar with the sight of it.

Have your helper stand between the shafts, pick them up, and begin to pull the cart around the ring as you drive the colt behind the cart. The colt will be a bit leary of the moving cart at first and unwilling to approach it while it is moving, but he will gradually gain confidence and soon you will be able to drive him up near it, pass by it, and

Figure 19. Cross-Country Cart.

circle around behind again. Drive him past the cart on both sides, halt him, and have the helper pull the cart past him. Repeat this performance until the colt will drive quietly along with the cart beside him but out of sight behind his blinkers. Make sure the helper shakes the cart to encourage any squeaks or rattles that are present so that the colt can become accustomed to the noise and be aware of its cause. The colt should be settled down after a few minutes of this type of work and be ready to be hitched in the cart. However, if the colt is still shying sideways from the cart, snorting and acting silly, he will have to continue the familiarization process a bit longer until he drives along quietly and under steady control.

It is advantageous at this point to expose your colt to the sight and sounds of another horse and cart being driven around the ring. If you can accomplish this, it will lessen the surprise later on when your colt is passed in the ring or on the road by such a turnout. Obviously, he has to get used to these sights and sounds, and the earlier you can expose colts to them, the easier it will be.

Hitching the Colt in the Cart

As before, position the cart at the end of the ring to allow the longest straight stretch before you have to turn. Drive the colt up past the left side of the cart and position him directly in front of the shafts. This is the manner in which he will be hitched from now on, and he should be driven up in this way each time. Have the helper attach the safety line to the halter and stand at his head. Bring the shafts up over the croup, then down and through the shaft loops. Put the traces on the singletree and check them for length. The shafts and traces should be fairly well in line now that he is in an actual vehicle. If the shaft is much lower than the trace, it will have to be raised up. The shaft at the front end should be just above the big muscle over the elbow. To raise it, you should take the colt out of the cart as it is a lengthy procedure, and you don't want your colt to have to stand and be subjected to the tugging necessary to get the buckle undone and the shaft loop raised. It is difficult to remove the tongue of these particular buckles because of the many thicknesses of leather used for the shaft loops.

When the adjustment has been completed, bring the cart up again, run the shafts through the shaft loops and put the traces on. Check that the tips of the shafts do NOT extend beyond the point of the colt's shoulder. This is adjusted by means of the traces. Next, the wrap straps must be put on, and now that the colt is in a cart these must be done properly to ensure their use as BRAKES. There should be a STOP on the shafts 12 to 15 inches

back from the tip, depending on the length of the shafts. On normal 6'3″ shafts, the shaft stop should be 14 inches back from the tip. The shaft loop should rest firmly in front of and against this stop. If there are no stops on your cart, you can install a pair of heavy shelving 'L' brackets as a temporary measure screwed onto the outside of your shaft back about 14 inches from the tip. If you do not install stops, you must use breeching or thimbles or there will be nothing to prevent the cart from sliding right up into the colt's rear quarters. THIMBLES are small leather cups which fit over the ends of the shafts and buckle back onto the backpad via a long strap. They act as stops by their bracing action. Thimbles are incorrect in the show ring in any class except Roadster. They do not work very well with a heavier cart and should only be used when nothing else is available.

Bring the wrap strap up between the trace and the colt and wrap over the shaft directly in front of the shaft loop (see Figure 10). Keep in mind as you put on your wrap straps that their purpose is to secure the shaft loop to the shaft and hold it firmly against the stop. Make one wrap in front of the shaft loop, then bring the strap back behind the shaft loop and wrap it around the shaft directly behind the stop. This will result in a figure-eight type of wrap. If you have enough length of strap to make two wraps on each side of the shaft loop, do so, but try to make them symmetrical on both sides of the horse. Bring the loose end down and buckle it back on to the lower end of the wrap strap, ending up with the trace between the straps. Do NOT wrap the trace with the wrap straps, just trap it in between, so that it can run freely. Go around to the other side and do up that side the same way. Be sure to keep the reins in your hand all the time you are working around a horse, hitching or unhitching. When changing sides, double the reins and fold them over his back, go around in front holding onto the reins near the bridle, then pick up the reins from the other side before you begin to adjust the harness on that side. If a horse spooks, jumps, or takes off part way through the hitching or unhitching process, there is no time to find and pick up the reins—you MUST always have them in hand. Your safety and the safety of others depend upon it. It is very easy to make the wrap straps too tight when buckling them down onto the lower end, due to the leverage gained over the shaft. Be careful that they are not tight enough to put excessive pressure on the backpad—they only need to be tight enough to hold the shafts from flopping. Usually after the wrap straps have been done up, the bellyband will need to be tightened a hole. Check this and the rest of the harness before moving off. Get in the habit at this stage of checking over all your harness before you move off. This is something you should always do for safety's sake as well as for appearance.

If you are using breeching with your harness, it must be attached and adjusted at this time. Make sure it is sitting on the flat part of the horse's rear quarters, down about 12 inches below the root of the dock. Bring the breeching strap under the trace and through the metal fitting under the shaft (footman loop), wrap it around the shaft as explained in the chapter on "adjustments," and buckle it back onto the breeching. Remember that the breeching straps should be done up so that there is about an inch or two of slack in them when the horse is moving forward. Check that both sides of the breeching are symmetrically done up and that the trace runs between the breeching straps. Again, do not wrap the trace, just trap it.

Adjust your reins, position yourself beside the cart in the same manner as in the poles, opposite the crossbar, and have the helper lead off the colt. Do *not* get into your cart yet! The colt must first get accustomed to the cart without your weight. You are driving and are in control, but the helper is giving the colt confidence by leading him the first few steps in this new piece of equipment. There should be no problems as you move off in the cart, because the sensation to the colt is almost the same as the poles. There will be a bit more weight on him downward through the shaft loops, depending on the type of cart used, but it will not be enough to bother him. If he has been going properly in the poles, the colt should go as well in the cart. The only real difference will be the noise that the cart may make, but if you have done the preparation well, the colt will realize quickly what is causing the noise and should not be too alarmed by it.

As with work in poles, the first corner is very important. If you can get around the first and second corners quietly, you are past the major stumbling block. You are driving the colt and will guide him around the corner, but your helper should be alert to assist with the turn should the colt not respond at once to your command. This way it is always possible to avoid becoming jammed in a corner and having to suddenly turn too sharply. It is imperative that you ask your helper for this assistance in time for its effect to be useful. Always *look ahead* and judge your distance from turns and like difficulties; it is too late to do anything if you wait until you are into them. The cart will turn much more readily than the poles because it rolls, so the turn should be easier for the colt than that to which he has become accustomed. By the time the second corner has been safely rounded, the helper should be able to drop back behind the blinkers and be relegated to safety man, in which case he does nothing but walk beside the colt keeping the safety rope readily in hand but under no contact, i.e. slack. Drive around on the track for a few rounds, halt and move on a few times allowing the colt to adjust to this new pull and weight. He will have to pull harder in the cart, and must lower his head slightly to lean into his breastcollar for the greatest ease of pulling. Reverse the ring, still using the large wide and smooth turns, and work the other way for a few rounds. You will not be able to slide back on your reins and cross over behind the cart as you were taught during work in poles. The cart is too bulky and the danger too great to attempt this maneuver unless you have a very low small cart. Halt the colt in the center of the ring on the diagonal, have the helper stand at his head, and fold the reins up over the colt's back in a manner that will make them easy to pick up from the other side. Walk around the front of the colt, pick up the reins and drive off from the new direction. Every time you change direction while walking beside the cart you will have to repeat this procedure. It is too cumbersome and almost impossible to retain steady and positive control of a horse otherwise. Begin to do circles and tighter turns with the cart, and when you feel the colt is going quietly you can mount into the cart. To do this, halt the colt at the end of the ring, have the helper stand at his head and step lightly into the cart from the right-hand side, as gently and unobtrusively as possible. The correct side from which the driver mounts into ANY horse-drawn vehicle is the *right*. The passenger mounts from the left. Dismounting is done in the same manner. Try to avoid excessive changes of weight on the colt from the shifting of your weight in the cart. Sit in the middle, as much in balance as possible, and adjust your reins in preparation for moving off. Sit up straight and keep that nice straight line from elbow to rein terret. Have the helper lead off the colt, then step back once his forward motion is established. Drive on the track making every effort to keep the corners smooth and large, and commend the colt with your voice now and then. Reverse the ring on the long diagonal and work the other way for a few rounds. By now it will be apparent whether or not the colt has accepted the new idea and if he is going quietly, the helper can take off the safety line and leave the driver to work SOLO. Remember that the colt has to work considerably harder to pull and balance the extra weight of your body and several rounds should be made with large and easy turns before attempting to tighten the circles. If you were to attempt difficult maneuvers before the colt has learned to manage the load properly, he might balk or refuse even to try, and this you must avoid. Give the colt at least one full lesson of easy work, i.e. following the track and easy large circles before asking him to do more advanced exercises.

Figure 20. Driving in a Cart. Top: Shanfara, the author's Arabian to a Cross-country cart. Bottom: Smokey, a Morgan-Quarter Horse cross to a metal cart. Smokey is owned by Shirlee Roma, Valleyford, Wash.

Taking the colt out of the cart requires careful and safety-oriented practices. Stop the colt in the middle of the ring and have the helper stand at his head as you unhitch. Keep the reins in one hand at all times. Unhitch in the exact reverse order of hitching. First undo the wrap straps and loop the free end back through its keeper making a tidy circular loop. Next undo and tie up the traces. Then slip the shaft loops as far as they will go forward on the shafts. Still holding the reins safely, pull the shafts and cart backwards out of the shaft loops and set the shafts on the ground. Now you can lead the colt forward and away from the cart with safety. Follow this practice each time you unhitch any animal from a vehicle. If breeching is worn, take the breeching straps off first as they were the last pieces of harness to be done up.

Work in the Cart

Gradually work the colt up to doing smaller circles, turns on the haunches, and smaller figure eights. Reassure him regularly and make a fuss over him when he does a new maneuver for the first time. After a few days in the cart, the colt should be able to circle smoothly and precisely in a small diameter of about 20 feet, should be able to execute turns on the haunches of 45 degrees easily and of 90 degrees with not too much difficulty, and should perform figure eights fluidly and knowledgeably. Do not keep doing figure eights or circles incessantly. The colt will become bored and sour. Vary his work as much as possible.

Check constantly to see that the colt is bending his head INTO his turns; he must not be allowed to tip his head to the outside. This is an all-too-common fault in driving horses, and the longer it is allowed to continue the harder it is to correct. The colt should also be made to stand for longer periods of time now that he is in a cart, and caution must be exercised that he does not try to back up to release the pressure of his breastcollar while he stands at rest. Although the poles could not move backward because of their nature, the cart can and will unless you prevent it quickly. The colt must never back unbidden and the idea must be quashed before it begins. Eventually, even on hills he must learn to lean into his collar, hold the cart in position, and not back off to release the pull on his chest. If he were to do this on hills, the cart would roll backward down the hill and, once the cart has started, the horse will *not* make any effort to hold it; he will just go with it, getting more and more panicky as it descends. In the show ring, he must also stay "up" in his traces in the line-up. The judge will be watching for little faults such as backing off the breastcollar.

The colt is now ready to begin to work at faster paces. The first few lessons at the trot should be done on the track quietly, varying the pace constantly from slow trot to walk and back to trot again (see Figure 20). At the trot, the cart is another new experience for the colt. It feels different at the trot, as it goes up and down with every stride and creates a greater force on his back. At a faster speed, the cart will likely make more noise too, so the colt has to adjust to this new situation before he is asked to do intricate movements at the trot. With each successive lesson the colt should be asked to do something new or harder, and soon he will be performing circles, figures, and variations in speed with ease and confidence. He will also be developing stronger muscles and greater balance and at this stage his checkrein will likely need to be readjusted up a hole or two to set his head carriage in the desired position. Check the martingale as well because the colt's chin should have come in as he worked up on the bit, and the martingale may have to be readjusted.

Advanced Work in the Cart

With his increase in knowledge and the build-up of his muscles, the colt can now be asked to push on at a faster trot until he has reached the ultimate gait of his breed, be it extended trot or high-stepping round action (see Figure 26). Vary the speed constantly, i.e. do not go around the ring at an extended trot, round after round, for this does not teach the colt anything. It is now that the colt's responses must be developed to the point where he moves instantly upon command, whether it be faster or slower, and this is accomplished in part by constantly changing the speed.

From now on you are working to put a "finish" on this colt, and he can be asked to collect himself more and more and move off his hocks as you work at the slower gaits as well as at speed. He should now be able to make his turns at a medium speed with good form, animation, and ease. His halts should be square, straight, and immediate, i.e. NOT ten feet after he was asked to halt. By this time the colt should be able to stand quietly in the cart for up to five minutes at a time. Now also, he should be made to stand the way he will be required to in the show ring. He must stand squarely, erectly, and easily; yet be alert to move off instantly upon command. All the colt needs now is lots of practice and exposure to all sorts of noises, traffic, and new situations.

Backing Up

After a couple of months work in the cart, the colt can be taught to back up and to maneuver the cart in reverse. Backing up is not a usual or pleasant maneuver for a horse. In the wilds, he escaped predators and dangerous encounters by wheeling and running. Thus, it is relatively easy to teach pivots, rollbacks, and pirouettes to a saddle horse. But rarely did a horse resort to backing up; a clumsy, awkward action for his conformation. So, now that we require his ability in that direction, we must teach him patiently and in a manner that he will understand and come to do willingly if not enjoyably. Start the colt backing up with just the halter on, standing in front of him and saying "back up" out loud to him, as you push back on the shank. Soon he will associate the word with the act and will back up upon command with very little pressure on the halter shank. Now put the harness on him with an open bridle (no blinkers) and using the verbal command, gently pull back on the reins at the same time. Use the PULL AND RELEASE system, rather than one steady big pull. This establishes the system of control for future use, where he will back up with the pull and stop with the release, thereby making it easy to regulate the number of steps he takes backwards. When the colt responds with a step to the rear, praise him, pat him and drive forwards for a short distance, then halt and repeat the procedure. Gradually he will back up for three or four steps, and no more should be asked of him for a few days until this becomes a quiet and willing habit. He must not be rushed or he will learn to back erratically, rushing backwards uncontrollably and crookedly. He must always be made to back up straight! Backing crookedly may not damage anything while hitched to a two-wheeled cart, but will jackknife and break a four-wheeled buggy in short order. Once the colt is backing up readily in the open bridle, put the driving bridle on and repeat the previous lessons. After the colt has backed the required number of steps, always make him walk forward up to his previous position and stand properly. This is a show ring requirement, but it is also good practice to establish in the colt's mind that the backing-up process is a short one always followed by forward movement. Backing up five or six different times in the driving bridle is sufficient practice for the colt if he is doing it easily and quietly.

Now hitch the colt to the cart, drive around a bit walking beside it, and then halt in the center of the ring. Before he settles completely, i.e. before loss of all impulsion, ask him to back up a couple of steps and then go forward immediately. Reward him with your voice or a pat, drive on again and repeat the lesson. Gradually the colt will learn to brace against the backpad and crupper (via the shaft loops, wrap straps, and stops) and will be able to back the cart up with ease and regularity. Get into the cart and go through the procedure again, asking for only a couple of steps backwards the first few times and working up to the number you wish. After a couple of weeks of backing up, the colt should be responding instantly and willingly and you can proceed to maneuver in reverse. Never carry on the backing-up lessons for long

periods of time, and only ask him to back up once from any one "halt." If the lesson lasts 30 minutes, I would not ask the colt to back more than three or four times in all. Despite understanding the process, horses do not like backing up very much as it is contrary to their nature and conformation. Therefore, it should be used only when necessary once the ability is firmly established.

The colt should be able to back the cart into the BUGGY SHED, and like situations. To teach this, put two rails down in the ring, parallel and about eight feet apart. The object is to back the cart between these rails evenly and without touching them. The rails simulate the walls of the buggy shed, without the danger of damage while both colt and driver learn this new skill. The advantage of knowing the turn on the haunches will be immediately obvious. It is the only way to execute a smart and accomplished parking job. Approach the rails at right angles and drive by the end selected as the opening, keeping as close as possible to reduce the distance that it will be necessary to back up. Halt the horse at the moment the cart is just past the midpoint of the opening and turn on the haunches AWAY from the rails until cart and horse are in line with and parallel to the rails, i.e. a 90-degree turn. Halt, settle the horse a moment, and then back slowly step by step between the rails until the cart reaches the "back" (see Figure 21). If this maneuver is done slowly, straightness can usually be maintained without major corrections. If the cart begins to go to one side, it can quickly be straightened again by a firm pull on the rein on that side. (The horse has to push the shaft around in a direction opposite to that in which you wish the cart to turn.) Considerable practice will be required to perfect this skill, and the onus is all on the driver! The horse will respond readily to directions, but it is up to the driver to give these directions at the precise moment and with just the right amount of force. It is well worthwhile to become skillful at this parking exercise, not only because of its usefulness but also as something with which to impress your friends. Better still, let them try it first and after they give it up as impossible then you can smugly (but modestly) show off! Practice this maneuver from both sides, so that you become equally dextrous. For some odd reason, this is always easiest when done from the left, and a driver may neglect to become proficient from the right.

Another Horse and Cart in the Ring
It is of great advantage (and lots of fun) to have another driving horse, preferably an experienced one, come to your ring to work with you and your colt. The colt will become accustomed to the sight and sound of another horse and cart and will learn to pass and be passed quietly. You will learn to gauge distances and their variation

with speed, a skill which is so necessary when overtaking and passing another vehicle. You should always pass with a margin of safety to allow for any "wandering" on the part of the other vehicle, and must pull back in on the rail leaving ample room for the following horse and cart to continue at a constant speed. Never pull in directly in front of another horse in a manner which will force it to be checked violently and slowed down, thus losing form, action, and most likely temper! This is a sure sign of ignorance as well as a dangerous and unethical move. Before you move out to pass another vehicle, always look ahead and judge the probability of a large enough gap being available for you to get back in on the rail. You can't stay out in the middle of the ring indefinitely making small circles and hiding the competitors on the rail from the judges' view.

Practice reversing the ring from opposite ends of the ring with your friend. The rule when meeting another horse head on is to KEEP TO THE RIGHT. Remember this at all times and the uncertainty of the other vehicle's probable path is eliminated. If you judge your speed carefully, you can meet each other on the middle of the diagonal, adding a bit of precision and form to your driving session. Gradually reduce the size of the turns until the two of you are performing a figure eight in symmetrical drill formation. This type of "play" increases the flexibility and control of your colt, and puts you well on the way to becoming an adept "whip." (A whip is the technical term for a good driver.)

It is a good plan to practice the halts and backing in the company of another horse. Your colt must learn to stand still while other horses back up or go out for more rail work, and the place to begin is at home. All these patterns of behavior are evidence of good habits, and these must be taught at home, not in the show ring.

Road Work and Obstacle Driving

It is a restful change of pace and scenery to do some road work with your colt. Start with a quiet back road or lane that has little traffic until your colt becomes accustomed to traffic. The changing scenery, traffic, mail boxes, and other different sights are very beneficial in your training program. They will spark vitality and interest, alertness and enthusiasm for his work. As well, he can be allowed to trot on at a greater speed without the worry of corners to turn every hundred feet or so. The colt will enjoy these sessions as much as you do and be much fresher and willing when back in the ring again. You must be alert at all times to possible hazards and causes for shying. Dogs running out barking, blowing scraps of cloth or paper, big rocks, reflections on puddles, and many other possible hazards must be constantly noticed and proper action taken in time.

Driving through a course of obstacles is a learning experience both for the horse and the driver. Set up a course of "gates" using plastic cones, in a manner that requires difficult and very careful calibration and control. Right-angle turns, sweeping curves, instant response to rein commands, fluid rein messages, and the fun of successfully negotiating such a course will be an ample reward. For a young colt, 15 or 16 such "gates" are sufficient.

Chapter Seven

Hitching the Colt In a Four-Wheeled Buggy

If the instructions in the previous chapters have been followed thoroughly, hitching the colt in a four-wheeled buggy should present no problems. I prefer to drive the colt in a cart for two or three months first but if there is a pressing reason why the colt must be hitched in a four-wheeled buggy after just a few weeks in the cart, it can be done safely. By then, the colt has become proficient in all the requirements of a driving horse, and a good rapport has been established between him and his driver. Each has confidence in the other and the driver will be better able to predict the behavior of the colt in any new or chance encounter.

Hitching in the buggy does not require the safety procedures which must be followed in the training for previously described vehicles. The colt is now trained to drive and understands most of the strange sounds, sights, and pulls connected with his work. There is no longer any need to be overly quiet or protective. Drive the colt up past the buggy on the left side and halt him in front of the shafts. Keeping the reins in hand, pull the shafts up over his croup and down through the shaft loops as usual. Check the traces for length so that the shaft does not extend past the point of his shoulder. Check that the traces and shaft are in line and adjust the shaft loop as necessary. When adjusted properly, the traces are usually almost completely hidden by the shafts on a buggy. In a four-wheeled buggy, the shafts will be nearly parallel to the horse's top line (and to the ground) due to their construction. Buggy shafts are completely independent of the buggy, in contrast to a cart's shafts which are directly connected and support it. Buggy shafts usually have almost a ninety-degree bend downwards at the singletree and crossbar (called drop heel shafts) to make them high enough to be parallel when through the

shaft loops. There is no weight on the horse in buggy shafts as the buggy is balanced on its four wheels, and the shafts function only as a means of turning. Do up the wrap straps, wrapping them in the figure-eight technique described earlier.

Now the colt is hitched and ready to go (see Figure 22). Check all the harness as you walk around from left to right via the head, pick up the reins and whip, and mount into your buggy from the right-hand side. Adjust the reins comfortably in your hands and move off. Stay on the track for awhile till both you and the colt get the feel of the buggy. The buggy will be another new experience for the colt. It will feel a little different to him as it does NOT go up and down with his strides as did the cart. Being balanced on four wheels and having independent shafts, the ride and pull are both smooth. If it is a show buggy, it will be considerably lighter than the cart. The colt will notice this and may be inclined to go with more spirit because of the easier pull. There is no difference to him in turning except that the buggy should be easier to turn having no great weight on its front wheels.

Precision Exercises

Drive on the track, reversing the ring frequently until your proficiency increases and you begin to feel at home in the buggy. Start doing circles and tighten them up gradually interspersing them with figure eights and serpentines. These exercises are designed to teach you where the front wheels are without having to look down to see. A poor impression is created in the ring if you always look down to find where the wheel is so that you may steer accordingly on turns. It is the sign of a poor driver or one with very little experience. You should be able to tell where your wheels are by the position the horse is in and the feel of the buggy under you. All that is required is

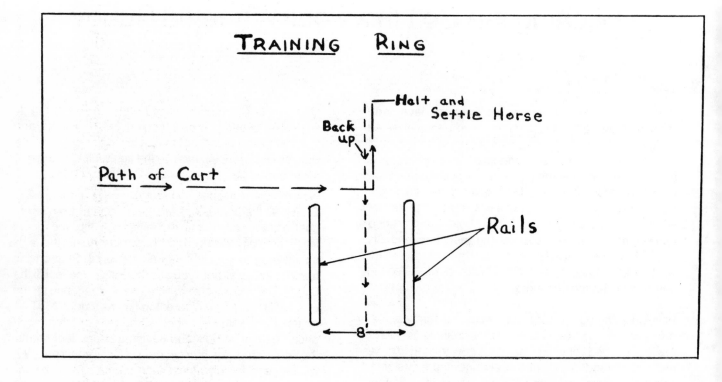

Figure 21. Backing between Rails.

Figure 22. Colt hitched to a Four Wheeled Buggy. Two year old Saddlebred, owned by the author.

practice and common sense—about equal amounts of each! With practice, you will be able to turn so sharply that the wheel is just a fraction of an inch away from jamming on the roller, and you will know exactly where that wheel is at all times. Watch your front wheels as you turn and soon you will have a mental image that will change constantly and automatically with the position of the horse, almost like your own personal RADAR system.

The sharpness of turns is restricted in a four-wheeled buggy due to its construction. You will not be able to execute a 90-degree turn on the haunches, but you can do a 45-degree turn, a maneuver that will be of great advantage in entering and leaving a line-up in the show ring.

Practice small circles, figure eights and passing procedures until you can perform them all with ease and smoothness. A circle should be round, not hexagonal, and you must be alert in a buggy to keep it round. Look at a constant point in the middle and drive a circle around it, looking ONLY at the center point. Figure eights should be smooth, positive and fluid, not jerky, erratic and uneven—again, more difficult in a buggy than in a cart. Figure eights should be even, i.e. both ends should match. Think of the pattern as being driven on a piece of paper that you will fold over at the middle point and the ensuing result should match perfectly. Passing procedures must be wide sweeping curves with positive judgement of space available, ie. you must know where the BACK WHEELS are as you swing back into position on the rail.

Backing Up

And now comes the challenge—backing up a four-wheeled buggy! Backing up straight in a four-wheeled buggy is not an easy task for the novice. Fortunately, in the show ring you are never required to back up any great distance. Usually three or four steps back is all the judge requires. The object is not to see how far you can back up, but how easily and willingly the horse performs this maneuver. The big secret of backing up straight in a buggy is to come into line absolutely straight in the first place. Make sure that your wheels are directly in line and that the horse is square and straight in front of the buggy when you halt. In this manner, it is fairly easy to back up straight for a short distance. However, if you come into line the least bit crooked, on the first step backwards the wheel will be well on its way to jam and jackknife the buggy. Crooked backing-up in a buggy shows up immediately as the horse and front wheels are in one direction and the box and remainder of the buggy are at a sharp angle to it. Backing up crookedly in a cart does not have the same unsightly appearance as things are still all in the same plane at least. Also, in a buggy once things get really crooked, the only way out of the mess is to go for-

ward first, straighten up horse and buggy and try again. With a well-trained sensible horse, slight amounts of "oscillation" can be corrected as he continues to back up. His ability to back up correctly will display the sound training you have given your colt. With the *pull-and-release system*, you can back up step by step, slowly and quietly, and can correct any slight movement to either side as it occurs. This is also the situation where a horse that rushes back uncontrollably gets into severe trouble—he can be neither steered nor stopped. You must remember to turn the horse in the OPPOSITE DIRECTION to achieve a correction in a four-wheeled buggy—exactly the opposite to the method used in the cart. For instance, if the left front wheel is getting a bit too close to the buggy (which means that the right one is too far out from the other side) as you back up, pull on the right rein to correct the direction. You must learn by trial and error how much pressure to exert and for how long; otherwise, you can end up with the right wheel too close as the horse turns too far. This maneuver is most easily done in between steps, i.e. when the horse is at rest for an instant, as this allows the sideways motion to end before the next backward motion begins. It is easier to avoid going into an oscillation from side to side if done in this manner, and also easier to gauge just when the horse is straight. You should practice getting in and out of situations like this, so that you can become proficient in extricating yourself smoothly. When you get into advanced obstacle driving, you will occasionally have to back through an "L" or a curved quarter-circle.

Advanced Work

Advanced work in the buggy should correspond to that done in the cart. The speed should be constantly varied to maintain maximum responsiveness and readiness. The horse will find it easier to maintain balance and cadence in the buggy with the freedom gained by the independent shaft arrangement. Work him with impulsion and collection for perhaps half a round. Try to avoid the habit of poking around the ring at the same speed all the time; the horse becomes bored and unresponsive and all presence and form is lost.

So now, with practice, patience, and perseverance your colt has made the journey all the way from nursery to show ring. He has made this journey quietly and progressively and at no time has he had his spirit broken or his faith in people shattered. He is now a fully trained and responsible driving horse in single harness and can be hitched with confidence and safety to any vehicle suitable for his type.

Your colt is ready now to start pair driving and, a little later on, tandem driving. He is also definitely ready for the show ring in single harness.

Figure 23. Viceroy Show Buggy, by Houghton (Ref. 5)

Figure 24. Fine Harness Show Buggy, by Houghton (Ref. 5)

Figure 25. Road Wagon, by Houghton (Ref. 5)

Chapter Eight

Types of Vehicles and Harnesses

Vehicles

There are literally hundreds of types of buggies, carts, and sleighs. In the "good old days" every manufacturer built his own style of buggy and named it, resulting in many different makes of buggies all closely resembling each other but with different names. Here in Canada there were many carriage manufacturers turning out buggies of similar appearance, but again, all with different names. The carriages in those days were much different and more elaborate than those one sees today. Victorias, Landaus, Barouches, Caleches and elegant Phaetons coursed along the streets doing the job of our cars today. Carriages in that age were a necessity and were built to the requirements of the era. They were certainly far different from our show buggies today, where their only purpose is to carry one person around a show ring for a few minutes. The history and development of carriages down through the ages are fascinating, and some of the types used in England in the early days are very interestingly depicted in Sally Walrond's book "Looking at Carriages" (Ref. 2) and "Carriage Terminology, an Historical Dictionary" by Don Berkebile (Ref. 3). The American counterparts are illustrated in great detail in "American Horse Drawn Vehicles" by Rittenhouse (Ref. 4), and "American Carriages, Sleighs, Sulkies and Carts" by Berkebile (Ref. 6). In winter time, sleighs were the mode of travel and their construction and variety were in direct relation to their purpose. While their decorativeness never quite equalled that of the carriages, some were very elaborate and luxurious. They boasted items such as bolsters, foot-warmers, robes and swansheads front—terms that some of our modern drivers would be hard pressed to identify.

In this book, we will only deal in detail with those vehicles normally available and in use today. Most of these vehicles are designed for a single horse and require no special skill other than that which you have arrived at in your training program. As far as the horse is concerned, the only difference in his sphere will be the difference in weight or noise of individual vehicles. His training is such that he can work equally well in any of them.

Buggies

For showing, the buggy you use will depend upon the breed of horse you have. For general use, any buggy of your choice is obviously the right one. Nearly every breed of horse is fitted, harnessed, and shown to a different type of vehicle. If you intend to show extensively, especially at recognized shows, you would be well advised to read a current copy of your national horse show association rule book (Ref. 7), which gives detailed rules and regulations concerning show equipment. "Drive On" by Doris L. Ganton (Ref. 8) also gives a very detailed and comprehensive look at these rules and regulations. For single driving horses, the most common show buggies are Viceroy, Fine Harness Buggies and Road Wagons, also called Caffrey Wagons. Viceroys are mainly used with Hackney horses or ponies (see Figure 23). Fine Harness Buggies are associated with American Saddlebred Fine Harness horses, Arabians and Morgans and are of the "side bar" type with rectangular box (see Figure 24). Road Wagons are used by Standardbred Roadsters and can be distinguished by their wooden spokes on an otherwise fairly standard light show buggy (see Figure 25). Shetland and Welsh ponies show in a variety of miniature Viceroys and Fine Harness buggies, as well as two-wheeled bikes (pony roadsters) and carts. Some breed classes are divided into "pleasure" and "formal" driving and, when this occurs, it is customary for the "pleasure" driving regulation to allow either two- or four-wheeled vehicles, whereas the "formal" driving stipulates a four-wheeled vehicle. At present, both Morgan and Arabian classes are divided this way.

Care of Buggies

Regardless of the type of buggy being used, the same consideration and care should be given to their maintenance and appearance. Wheels should be kept properly and regularly greased, spokes checked frequently for looseness, and nuts examined occasionally for safety as well as to prevent rattles that develop when they work loose. Shaft attachments should be checked for wear and all leathers such as trace guides and single tree retainers examined for cracks or weakened areas. The chrome should be kept well polished and the paintwork on the box and seat clean and protected with a light coat of wax. Cushion and floormat should be taken out and shaken or vacuumed regularly for appearance and maximum life. If possible, and especially if being transported frequently, canvas dust or shipping covers are very desirable to protect the buggy from wear and weather. Buggies and carts should be stored in a dry place with good air circulation. Mildew, rust, and dry rot regularly take their toll of horse-drawn vehicles.

If the upholstery is of real leather, clean it with a glycerine type of saddle soap, then, after wiping well, apply a coat of harness dressing. If it is black upholstery, a black harness dressing will work well, but if the carriage has tan or light-colored leather, a clear harness dressing will be required. Tops also can be maintained in the same manner. The wooden parts of a vehicle should be washed, dried, and well rubbed. A light spraying with "Pledge" and a subsequent polishing with a soft, dry cloth will achieve a beautiful deep shine that will repel dust for some time. For the brass parts, "Duraglit" has worked very well for the author. It is simple and not messy to use and achieves a beautiful shine without dirtying up the leather. A brisk rub with a soft cloth daily will maintain this shine for several weeks.

Sleighing

Winter time in most parts of the country brings snow and crisp cold weather, which most drivers are quick to take advantage of. Sleigh rides are great fun for everyone, including the horse. Whether you have a "one-horse open shay" pulled by old Dobbin, or an exquisite landau sleigh drawn by high-stepping Hackneys, the thrill is the same. Cold air and snow underfoot, coupled with the passengers' enthusiasm, seem to give added zest and spirit to the horse pulling a sleigh, and the result is a wonderful and lasting experience for the sleigh riders. With his breath hanging crystallized in the cold air, head and tail held proudly, and his hooves speeding soundlessly on the soft snow, the horse is truly a picture to behold! Horses always seem to enjoy their work in a sleigh and perhaps this is the reason they act in such a "show off" fashion.

There is no extra training required to teach your horse to pull a sleigh. If he is noise conscious, he will be aware of the difference in sound. The runners on snow make practically no sound at all, but if they break through to gravel or pavement for a few feet, very weird and high-pitched scrapes occur. The first time or two that this happens, the horse will likely start slightly but soon will just accept it as part of sleighing. Turning the sleigh around is no problem at all on a well-packed surface, but if attempted in deeper snow it is quite a chore for the horse who has to shove it around bodily due to its rigid construction. If this is necessary, it is wise to get down from the cutter or sleigh during the turn to make it easier for both horse and equipment. Sleigh bells are almost a necessity on a sleigh, for their cheerful sound gives the ride a real lilt and brightens up the whole route for passersby as well. Originally sleigh bells had another use: that of warning other vehicles of their approach at night or around very sharp turns on narrow roads.

A light cutter or sleigh requires no special harness or breeching, just the ordinary wrap straps against stops will do the job nicely. Naturally, if you are pulling a heavy load or driving in very hilly country, you will be well advised to use breeching, but experience and common sense should dictate these necessities. One word of caution for the driver— wear extra warm gloves! Holding reins in cold weather numbs your hands in minutes unless they are well protected. I prefer woollen-lined leather gloves myself and, as mentioned in the chapter on gloves, they must be a bit long in the fingers and loose. The reins and whip are held in the same manner in a sleigh as in a buggy. Warm lap robes are customary and very welcome while driving in a sleigh. Buffalo robes were worn in the early days, but these are virtually non-existant now and really unnecessary for our relatively short pleasure drives.

Another use for a well-trained driving horse in winter is for SKI JORING. Skiers each hold the end of a long rope attached to a bar or singletree and fan out behind the horse as he trots along a field or road. The horse is usu-

Figure 26. Hackney Horse to a Viceroy. "Ardinglas Marques", Champion Harness Horse at Toronto, Devon and Syracuse. Owned by Mr. & Mrs. Robert Weaver, Peoria, Illinois.

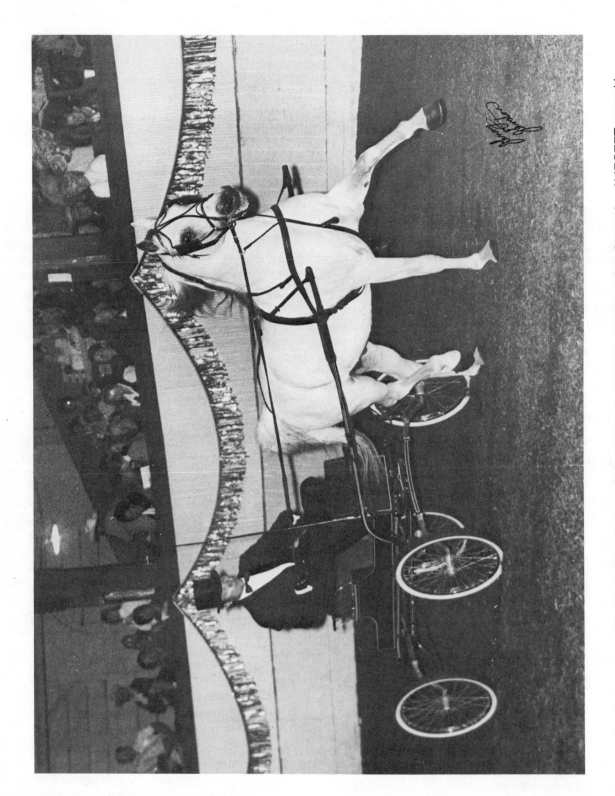

Figure 27. Arabian Formal Driving Horse. Many times U.S. and Canadian National Champion *MECZET owned by Ron and Joyce Palelek, Vantage, Washington.

ally ridden for this sport, with the driving breast collar and traces on as well as saddle and bridle. This is a very thrilling sport, and the skiers require expert balance and timing and the ability to laugh off a spill!

Harnesses

There are several distinct types of harness and many variations of single harness. As this book is devoted to a light breed of horse pulling a fairly light vehicle, I will not elaborate on the heavier types of harness used with Gigs, Tandems or other weighty vehicles.

As was the case with buggies, each breed of show horse also uses its own particular style of harness. Sometimes the difference is so slight as to be barely noticeable, but each breed has its own rule book and in it the required harness is designated (ref. 7 and 8). This should not lead you to the conclusion that any particular breed can be driven only in one style of harness. On the contrary, *any* breed can be driven in *any* harness, but for show purposes the breed committees have stipulated the harness type. This uniform arrangement makes it easier for a judge to do his job and eliminates the confusion and worry over choice. Quality is still a big factor, but in this respect price is usually a good criterion. You get what you pay for.

Good harness makers are few and far between these days, although in the past five years many new harness and carriage manufacturers have sprung up. You should examine the quality of the leather and workmanship carefully when choosing your set of harness. If chosen wisely, this set will last you for life given the proper care, so it is not a choice that should be rushed. A backpad with a spring steel tree will outlast the type with soft tufted pad, and keep its shape despite neglect in storage. Non-cracking patent leather costs a bit more than the other type, but will still look perfect in years to come. Solid brass hardware is preferable to brass plating which will wear off in a few years. Traces, checkreins driving reins, and wrap straps should be of a thickness directly in proportion to the rest of the harness. Reins with steel reinforcement where they buckle onto the bit are likely to last longer than the ordinary all-leather style. This is a dangerous WEAR AREA on reins and one that must be checked regularly for safety. Inspect these features and the overall appearance and quality of the set when you are shopping for your harness.

Getting down to the right type of harness required for each breed, we will begin with the Hackney. The harness used on Hackneys is very much in keeping with their elegant appearance and brilliant action. It has an abun-dance of patent leather and gleaming hardware of solid brass. Hackneys show in side checking bridles with round blinkers and either a Liverpool or a Buxton bit. Running martingales are never used on this breed. Their breast collars are of the folded and sewn type with buckle-on traces. The backpad is very fine and usually has French or Tilbury shaft loops. The crupper can be of ordinary type or spoon crupper style. No breeching is worn. All show reins should be black with tan hand parts, or all tan, and hand holds on reins are optional. Figure 26 shows a Hackney horse being shown properly harnessed to a Viceroy show buggy.

Fine Harness horses are of the breed called American Saddlebreds, and they show in a very fine, light harness which also has considerable patent leather enhancing it. The bridle is of the overdraw checkrein type with square blinkers and snaffle bit and a separate check bit. A running martingale is always used in conjunction with the snaffle bit. The breast collar should be of the folded and sewn type with buckle-on traces made round with flat ends. The backpad is narrow and fine with ordinary shaft loops and wrap straps. The crupper is either of the usual sewn-on type or the style with tail set. Reins are usually of round leather, either black with tan hand parts, or all tan. Hand holds are optional.

Arabians show in two categories: the Formal Driving class and the Pleasure Driving class. Formal Driving horses wear the same type and style of harness as the Fine Harness horse described above with ordinary crupper, and usually use sewn-on traces instead of the buckled on style. Figure 27 shows an Arabian Formal Driving horse hitched to a proper four-wheeled show buggy. The Pleasure driving Arabian usually wears a slightly heavier and stronger harness, but it is every bit as fancy. Backpad and crupper are of the ordinary light type with patent leather trim, and the hardware can be either brass or nickel. Reins are usually flat black leather with tan hand parts. Hand holds are not allowed in a Pleasure class. With the new 1982 regulation, Arabians are now allowed to wear side checks as well as overdraw style checkreins. Figure 20a shows an Arabian of Pleasure type put to a Cross Country cart. The cover photo also shows a Pleasure driving Arabian, just two years old, put to a restored Stud cart.

Morgans fall into the same two categories as Arabians and wear much the same harness. Morgans are allowed to wear snaffle, Liverpool or Buxton bits, and the accompanying proper type of checkrein. Figure 20b shows a Pleasure driving Morgan to a light Show cart.

Standardbred Roadsters are shown in extremely fine light harness. Bridles are of overdraw checkrein style with square blinkers. The breastcollar, with straight flaps and full martingale, should have round traces and is usually made up in a very narrow width. The backpad and crupper are similar to that worn in Fine Harness classes, but with ordinary sewn-on crupper. For appointment classes, breeching must be worn, and it too reflects the unusual fineness of this style of harness. All buckles on a Roadster harness should be leather or rubber covered and the reins should be made round up to the tan hand parts.

Standardbred Race Horses wear a light but very strong harness with no patent leather and either nickel or chrome hardware. Billets usually have a rawhide counterpart for safety and the end effect is two of each strap. Depending upon whether they are trotters or pacers, they wear different types of accessories. Pacers wear hopples to assist them in their lateral gait, and both trotters and pacers at times wear an assortment of boots and other gear specific to their needs and way of going. Nylon and plastic harness is becoming more popular with race drivers as it requires much less care and cleaning. It can just be hung on the harness hook and hosed clean.

Care of Harness

The care you take of your harness will be reflected in its appearance and longevity. Harness should be wiped dry after each use and if it becomes gummed up with sweat or dirt, it should be cleaned with a good saddle soap. When cleaning harness, the sponge should be fairly dry with a good thick lather of soap; always try to avoid excessive wetness in cleaning. Dry off the leather immediately, and if it has become cracked or very dried out and dull, an application of harness oil and black harness dressing will give it new life and appearance. Show harness keeps its appearance and stays clean and shiny best when stored in a harness bag, a drawstring type of rectangular bag made of a heavy duck or breathable canvas material. Harness bags are almost an essential item at horse shows where the dust continually settles thickly on everything. The patent leather on your harness will benefit from an occasional light application of vaseline, rubbed in well and the excess wiped off. The brass hardware should be inspected regularly and kept in good condition. Brass tarnishes very easily. On the other hand, nickel hardware requires practically no maintenance except for an occasional wipe and polish. The crupper merits special and daily care to ensure that it is absolutely clean and soft—the tail head can be scalded or galled very quickly by a crupper that is rough and cracked or has dirt encrusted on it. As you clean your harness, check for wear spots, cracks, rotted sewing, or other potentially dangerous weak areas. Proper care of your harness will result in safe driving for you and comfort for your horse.

Chapter Nine
Hints And Happenings

Hazards

One of the most common hazards of driving is a horse getting his tail over the rein. This situation applies to seasoned horses as well as colts, and if not dealt with quickly and competently can develop into a dangerous kicking or bolting action. It is very frightening to a horse to have this situation occur and it can happen in a flash. The horse flicks his tail in a circular swish at a fly and as it comes down it catches the rein underneath. The horse immediately clamps down on the rein, tucks his tail and quarters and behaves erratically if the rein is not removed at once. If you see the tail come down over the rein, immediately give a voice command of "whoa" but do NOT pull on the reins. Try to free the rein from under the tail. If you are in a cart, this is fairly easy as you can lean forward and lift the tail off the rein (always lift the tail from below the bone to prevent even tighter clamping on the horse's part) and as the rein falls free you can pick it up and resume control with no damage done. If you are in a four-wheeled buggy, this is sometimes impossible, especially if the horse is hitched fairly long. You will either have to rely on the voice command or leap out of your buggy and go to his head. Whatever you do, NEVER pull on the rein that is under his tail—this makes the problem much worse, creating more pressure on the undertail area and prompting the horse to resist even more. To pull on the free rein is of no help, as all it can do is turn him. As he turns, he will automatically put pressure (pull) on the trapped rein, ending up again in more trouble. The answer, of course, is to avoid the tail-over-the-rein situation altogether by being alert all the time. If you know your horse is a switcher—and some are much worse than others—you should be doubly alert. As you see your horse begin to switch his tail, carry your reins wide by separating your hands; then resume their normal position when the tail is again at rest. Sometimes it helps to carry the hands a bit higher as well as wider for that instant. This depends to a large extent on the length of the horse's tail bone. In fly season, you should use a good fly spray or wipe to help the switching problem, and keep in mind the potential hazard all the time you are driving. If all else fails, braid and tie the end of the tail to the center of the singletree. Be sure to leave some slack in the twine or rope with which you tie it; do not make it so tight that the horse cannot move his tail at all.

Breakage of harness is always a hazard and sometimes happens despite frequent inspections and proper upkeep and care. The seriousness of the breakage depends entirely upon the function performed by the piece of harness involved. The thing to do in any case is to stop the horse as quickly as possible and in a manner that will not excite him. This is where voice commands and confidence in his driver will come to the fore and can save the day (and the equipment!).

Never push a cart or vehicle with old-fashioned style hubs—grease-bearing style axles—*backwards* for any distance. A wheel can fall off! This style of vehicle has all the nuts tightening towards the front, i.e. the nuts on the left side have a left-hand thread (counter clockwise to tighten) and the nuts on the right side have a right-hand thread (clockwise to tighten). These old-style axles have no cotter key to prevent the nut from unthreading and, if pushed backwards, especially over rough ground where a slight bump can loosen it, the nut may come nearly all the way off. Then when the vehicle goes forward, the nut, being already loose, may fall right off, followed by the wheel. Don't worry about short back-ups with these vehicles; they will not cause any problem if the nuts were tightened properly when put on. But avoid using them as you would a wheelbarrow—holding the shafts as handles to push them backwards. If a wheel falls off after you have hitched your horse and are driving off, a serious accident can occur.

A checkrein bouncing off the hook at speed can sometimes create a difficult situation. As a horse speeds up, his head automatically is held higher, thus loosening the checkrein. This action is often enough to bounce the leather retainer (tab), in which the hole has perhaps become enlarged, off the checkrein hook, and the head at once is free and unsupported. This can be very disturbing to a horse that has always been accustomed to its support and whose balance and manner has been developed in conjunction with a certain fixed head carriage. It is wise to check this leather retainer from time to time, and see that it is hooked on firmly when in use.

Never take the bridle off a horse while he is hitched to a vehicle. This little action has caused innumerable accidents right down through the ages. Unhitch the horse, take him to his usual cross-ties, hitching post or wherever he is normally tied to be groomed, harnessed etc., THEN remove the bridle and harness. Removing the bridle allows the harness horse to suddenly see the vehicle behind him. Perhaps it moves or he sees it from a strange angle, but the result is always the same—he panics, bolts, and usually runs away with the vehicle STILL attached! Even if you have a halter on the horse, you will be hard-pressed to hold him; he is much stronger than you and, in his state of panic does not listen to your commands. A horse running loose with a vehicle attached is an uncontrolled weapon of disaster; the vehicle will veer from side to side, wiping out cars, people, anything in its path. The horse will run faster and faster, bucking and kicking in his frantic efforts to be rid of "the monster chasing him." It is very difficult to stop such a runaway, as you are in danger of being skewered by the shafts, if not knocked down by the rocketing vehicle and terrified horse. Often, the horse is not badly hurt physically, but these disasters usually end in a complete wreck with damages to cars, property, and people reaching astronomical amounts. These frightening episodes can be avoided easily with proper unhitching procedures and common sense. DO NOT EVER take the bridle off before unhitching the horse!

Do not leave a horse and carriage unattended. No matter how quiet you believe him to be, nor how short the errand contemplated, *never* leave him alone. Anything can happen to spook him in those short moments, and with Murphy's Law in mind—"anything that can go wrong, will!"—it is like playing Russian roulette. If the errand is that important and you are alone, unhitch the horse, tie him up, do your errand, then rehitch. The time this takes is well worth the effort in view of the likelihood he may run off hitched to the vehicle. Never take chances with such very important aspects of carriage driving. While on the subject, never tie a horse *hitched* to a vehicle by the bridle. I consider it completely unsafe to tie him at all if he is still hitched but, if you must, put a sturdy halter on over the bridle and tie him short and securely. When you leave him tied in this manner, don't go far away and do keep checking on him. He can get himself into a lot of trouble quickly and if he panics and breaks the shank, you have a colossal runaway on your hands.

These hazards can be easily avoided with diligent alertness. They are listed merely to make the reader aware that they exist, and being aware of them to see that they do not occur. With lots of practice under varying conditions, a driver automatically does the right thing without consciously thinking of it, and hazards come into this sub-conscious category.

Always carry a few spares when you go driving. A hame strap, some baler twine, a knife and wheel wrench will allow most repairs to be done to get you back home.

Driving Techniques

Everyone develops his own individual style of driving in time, and to a great extent he applies this technique to all the horses he drives. Driving technique varies from breed to breed as regards the manner in which the horse is shown, but the basic style varies very little. The important thing is to develop your driving technique to the point where it is natural and effective and at the same time pleasing to watch. Sitting erectly in the center of the buggy seat, holding the reins and whip properly, and conducting the horse around the ring efficiently at the gait called for presents a very pleasing picture of competence. Being constantly alert for changes of gait called for and gaps on the rail you can utilize, gives you the opportunity to show your horse to a much greater advantage. Keep one eye on the judge and try to anticipate his requests—this allows you just that bit of extra time necessary to prepare your horse for the change in gait or direction. When a reverse is called for, do it smartly and do it ACROSS THE RING. Never try to turn around in a circle to reverse in a buggy! The proper way is to reverse the ring on the diagonal, but if this is not convenient, at least cross the ring on a bit of an angle

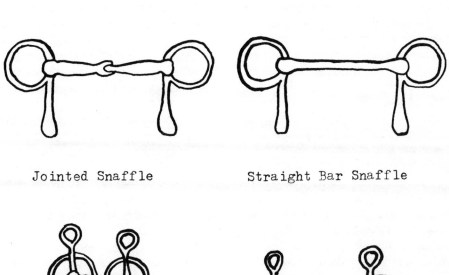

Jointed Snaffle   Straight Bar Snaffle

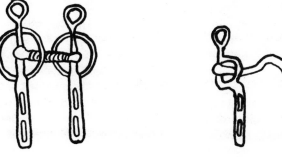

Liverpool Bit   Elbow Bit

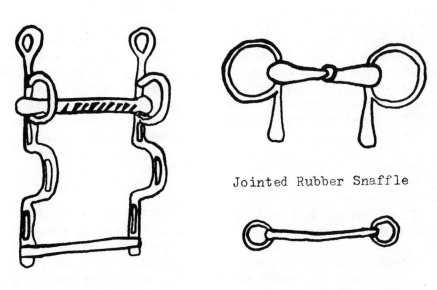

Buxton Bit   Straight Overcheck Bit

Figure 32. Some Driving Bits.

and enter the track smoothly in the new direction. Always keep alert to the actions of the other competitors; it is quite easy to end up in a pile-up in the middle of the ring. In some shows, the Ringmaster will indicate where he wishes the reverse to be initiated, and in that situation there is no problem or choice. When the order to "Line Up" is called, drive into line as quickly as possible. Don't dawdle around the ring keeping the judge and everyone else waiting. Line up as straight as possible, leaving enough room on each side of your horse for the judge to walk between horses safely and for him to see your horse to its best advantage. Sit straight and look straight ahead—don't goggle around at the other competitors or the judge. Above all, *don't* talk to your neighbors. Not only does it divert your attention from your horse, but it looks terrible. Save your chats and conversations for outside the show ring; they have no place in the ring. Hold your reins in a relaxed manner but in a way that will allow you to take hold of your horse instantly should it be necessary. In other words, look and be alert, proud, and competent.

Bits and Bitting

While the most common bit to be seen in single harness is the half cheek snaffle, there are many other types and it is sometimes a lengthy process to find the proper "key" to a particular horse's mouth. Bitting is mainly a matter of common sense and experience. Whatever type is used, it should lie flat in the horse's mouth, about one inch above the tusks and should be no more severe than necessary.

Arabians, Fine Harness Saddlebreds and Roadsters are required by their breed rules to wear snaffle bits. Hackneys usually wear Liverpool or Buxton bits, or sometimes Elbow bits (see Figure 32). These bits have a curb chain or strap attached and it should not be too tight. It should allow two fingers width between it and the horse's jaw.

For a very light-mouthed horse, a snaffle with a rubber mouthpiece often works very well, or, if this is unavailable, covering an ordinary snaffle with leather will make a good substitute. A double ring, or Wilson snaffle, is sometimes the answer to bitting problems in this direction.

For pullers, there are many bits and devices that give varying results. A confirmed puller will invariably get used to any bit, and the answer in this case is to change bits frequently. A Liverpool bit usually works well for a puller with its four positions of adjustment for leverage. For a horse that gets his lip over the end of the bit constantly, an Elbow bit is a good preventative, while retaining the leverage effect of a curb bit. Good hands are often a much better cure than any severe bit. Force begets force and the more you pull on a horse, usually the more he pulls.

For a side puller, or a horse that leans his head out to one side constantly, a bit burr is sometimes effective. This consists of a circular piece of leather with a round hole in the middle and a slot to the outside to allow easy attachment and removal. It has stiff nylon bristles on the side next to the horse's mouth and discourages the horse from leaning into it. If a commercial burr is not easily obtained, one can be made from an ordinary round cheek leather with a few tacks pushed through it. As side-pulling very quickly becomes a habit, it should be straightened up as soon as possible.

A very practical and widely used bit is the overdraw checkbit. It is a slim, small-ringed bradoon, either jointed or straight, that attaches to the checkrein. Some horses work much better when their checkreins are attached to this type of separate bradoon rather than onto the snaffle which also is the attachment point for the cheek straps and reins. For best results and lasting finish, a stainless steel checkbit with one-inch rings is recommended.

Only so much can be accomplished using bits; the biggest results are obtained using your HANDS. Hands have a mystic quality that allows one person to handle and control a horse with the utmost ease and sympathy, while another person may have nothing but difficulties and lack of control. Hands, contrary to the old adage, are NOT always born and CAN be made. With proper teaching and practice plus lots of experience, hands can be developed to the subtlest degree, and, in many cases, good hands can control a difficult horse with the mildest of bits. While severe bits are sometimes genuinely necessary, it is frequently a case of poor hands.

Work with a Rein Board is a good exercise to achieve and retain good hands.

Appointments and Attire

Appointments are the items required to be included as equipment in certain classes. They vary from class to class and from breed to breed. The best source of information on this subject is your national Horse Show Association.

Attire, too, varies from class to class and helpful information may be obtained from the same source. The main thing is to always be dressed neatly and quietly. Gaudy

Figure 28. Roadster to a Caffrey Road Wagon. "Jeannie's Nan Cee", Royal Winter Fair Winner, Toronto. Owned and driven by Bill Malcomson, Barrie, Ontario.

Figure 29. Pair Hackney Horses put to a Ladies Phaeton by Brewster. Owned and driven by Mrs. Anne Wakefield-Leck, Wayzata, Minnesota.

Figure 30. Pair Morgan Horses. "Otterbrook Alida and Greene Acres Debbie" consistent champions in competitive driving events. Owned by Mr. & Mrs. Philip DuBois, Peterborough, N.H. and driven by Peter Morin.

Figure 31. Pair Standardbred Roadsters. "Royal Arian and Jeannie's Nan Cee", Champion pair, Royal Winter Fair 1978. Owned and driven by Bill Malcomson, Barrie, Ontario.

Figure 33. Four-in-Hand of Hackneys beautifully turned out to a vis-a-vis sleigh. Owned and driven by Mrs. Anne Wakefield-Leck, Wayzata, Minnesota.

Figure 34. Tandem of Morgans, properly harnessed and moving with great form in the Dressage Test. "Otterbrook Alida and Greene Acres Debbie", 1980 and 1982 Newport Carriage Festival Champions. Owned by Mr. & Mrs. Philip DuBois, Peterborough, N.H., driven by Peter Morin. (Note the use of tandem bars)

Figure 35. Unicorn of Hackneys to a Demi Mail Phaeton by Brewster. Correctly harnessed, hitched and turned out. Owned and driven by Mrs. Anne Wakefield-Leck, Wayzata, Minnesota.

colors have no place in most driving classes in the show rings of today. Hat and gloves should always be worn, and at times a lap robe is indicated. Neatness and choice of attire reflects the pride you have in your turnout and creates a favorable impression in the ring. In classes where it stipulates "Lady to Drive," the lady should look like one and wear a dress rather than saddle suit or jodphurs. One often hears the complaint, "Oh, it's too much bother to change into a dress." In that case, why "bother" to enter the class at all! I feel we should try to maintain the heritage and quality of our driving classes and preserve their pageantry—not let them degenerate into a caricature.

Teams and Tandems

Driving a pair (two horses side by side) or a tandem (two horses, one in front of the other) is an art in itself, and requires a different type of harness and vehicle. "Hints on Driving" by Captain C. Morley Knight (Ref. 9) has some interesting and informative chapters on these modes of driving as does "Drive On" (Ref. 8) by Doris L. Ganton.

Figure 34 shows a Tandem of Morgans, while Figure 30 depicts a pair. A pair of Hackneys put to a Ladies Phaeton is shown in Figure 29, while Figure 31 depicts a pair of Standardbred Roadsters shown to a Road Wagon, a very different type of turnout.

Then there are Unicorns, Four-in-Hands and Six- and Eight-horse teams. A unicorn is a pair of horses in the wheel with one single leader out in front. Figure 35 shows a very beautiful unicorn of Hackney Horses put to a Demi Mail Phaeton.

Four-in-hands—two pairs in tandem—are becoming more numerous in recent years. Figure 33 shows a four-in-hand of Hackneys put to a vis-a-vis sleigh, impeccably turned out. Four-in-hand coaching classes have become very popular in some areas, especially with the advent of World Championship three-phase event driving competitions. Prince Phillip, H.R.H. The Duke of Edinburgh, was instrumental in forming the four-in-hand competitions and setting up subsequent F.E.I. rules. His new book "Competition Carriage Driving" will be of considerable help and interest to whips in this rather advanced stage of driving. Figure 39 shows a picture of H.R.H. The Duke of Edinburgh driving the Dressage test at the World Championships in 1982.

The six- and eight-horse hitches are usually of heavy draft horses—Clydesdales, Percherons or Belgians—and are very popular at shows and fairs. It is always a thrill to watch a teamster put his six- or eight-horse hitch

through its paces. In some cases, he seems to have less trouble and more control than another man driving a single horse! Figure 40 shows a Six-horse team of Champion Belgians.

Driving Outside the Ring

Fields, trails and quiet roads make a nice change of scenery for both horse and driver after a concentrated period in the training ring. Great pleasure can be derived from these excursions into the countryside as well as providing further and valuable training of the horse. Long straight stretches of road allow the horse to be driven at speed for a much greater distance than is possible in a ring, and balance, cadence and unrestrained freedom of movement are a few of the benefits gained. The exhilaration and enjoyment that the driver experiences is the *raison d'etre* of driving.

The driver must be constantly aware—usually subconsciously—of his surroundings and the possible reactions of his horse to objects encountered along the way. Cars, mail boxes, blowing paper, and many other objects are potential trouble sources, and the alert driver spots these things well in advance and guides his horse accordingly. If you see something ahead that you think will cause your horse to shy and perhaps be difficult to pass safely, it is often a good idea to put your horse into a good trot before reaching the object and in this way keep his attention diverted as he trots on by. A slight twitch of the hand to set his head slightly away from the object in question also helps the maneuver. Quite often what he can't see doesn't scare him.

Rein guides are very useful for pleasure driving. These are small curved metal pieces molded onto a Conway loop fitting that thread onto the loin straps of the breeching. They are just high enough to keep the rein from slipping down to shaft level where it invariably gets hung up on the lower end of the loin strap billet. They allow the driver to relax more as the tension can be maintained easier, and if suddenly he must use the reins, they are right in position. These rein guides should be positioned on either side of the crupper strap equally, down about eight inches on the loin straps, or where ever they sit well to accomplish the job.

When driving out on the roads, the driver must keep an eye on the nature of the shoulder he is travelling. Sometimes it disappears suddenly in a wash-out or a culvert and you have to swerve out onto the road to avoid going over the edge. Always remember to look behind and check that you are not swerving out into the path of a following car. It is also a good idea not to drive on the shoul-

Figure 36. Pleasure Driving Horse to a Ralli Car. "Pebble Bay", Quarter horse cross, Eastern U.S. Pleasure Driving Champion 1981. Impeccably turned out, correct to the last detail. Owner/Whip: Patricia A. James, Modesto, California.

Figure 37. Hackney Pony to a Basket Wicker Phaeton by McLaughlin. "Special Magic", Champion pleasure and show pony in 1976. Owned and driven by the author.

ders (or roads) at night unless you are very familiar with them. I can remember my own rather disastrous experience in this regard and although it seems humorous now, it was certainly not funny at the time. I was enroute to Shawville, Quebec from Arnprior, Ontario and, having no trailer in those days, I was driving my mare, Lucky, in the show buggy the whole way. The trip involved a ferry ride across the Ottawa River. For some forgotten reason, I had undertaken this trip in the early evening which meant that the remainder of the trip had to be done in the dark. We disembarked from the ferry (an experience in itself with a horse and buggy!) with vague directions but enthusiastic good wishes from passengers and crew. I had my dear old Hackney mare, Lucky, in the shafts of the show buggy and all my saddles and equipment necessary for a three-day stay plus my shaggy terrier, Patch, piled up high in the tiny vehicle. All went well for the first hour or so as Lucky picked her way along the shoulder of the highway. I left the route entirely up to her once we were established on the shoulder in the right direction as it was so pitch dark I could just occasionally distinguish the fence posts off to my right. Singing gaily (mostly to reassure myself), the miles seemed to go by very slowly, and the lack of traffic was an unspoken worry that perhaps we were on the wrong road. When finally a car came along and its headlights illuminated a sign—Shawville—4 miles—my relief was tremendous. Feeling that the worst was behind me, I clucked Lucky into a brisk trot meaning to make good time on those four miles. All of a sudden, it seemed the bottom of the world fell out from under us, and the next instant we were all upside down in a ditch! The shoulder had been washed out for about 10 feet at that point, and in the darkness even Lucky had been unable to see it. The mare scrambled to her feet first, righting the buggy as she came up, moved off a few steps uncertainly, snorting and shaking. Even though thoroughly frightened and bruised, she obeyed my muffled "whoa" from underneath the load of equipment and stood stock still till I was able to extricate myself and go to her head. The only permanent damage was a broken shaft, which I spliced with a handy stick and some baling twine. I loaded all the scattered equipment and my very shaken dog back into the buggy (no mean feat in the dark) and continued my trip without further incidents into Shawville and to the Fair Grounds. Although this accident occurred 30 years ago, it remains indelibly stamped on my mind and comes to the surface often when I am driving on the roads.

It is a refreshing change for your horse to get out of the ring occasionally. Horses that are worked continually in a ring often become "ring sour" and lose their interest and animation, becoming dull and listless in their unending circling of the same area. Put yourself in their place and just think how bored you would become. This is often the explanation of a poor workout or otherwise unsatisfactory training session. Horses enjoy a change of scenery and the challenge of different terrain almost as much as their drivers and will return to their home rings ready to work with fresh vim and vigor.

When driving in an open field, the route should be followed at a walk initially to investigate the possibility of holes or rocks that might cause a serious accident if come upon at speed. Once the proposed path in a field has been found safe, working at various speeds is great fun and a wonderful source of muscling for your horse. It is in large fields or on open roads where you can establish the trotting habit firmly in your horse's mind. He should be encouraged to trot faster and faster until he is just on the verge of breaking into a canter, then brought back to a steadier speed. This will increase his ability to the point where he can trot at speed with no thought of breaking and will give you a positive understanding of his utmost ability. Horses should not be allowed to canter in a buggy until very well trained. When they break into a canter they should be pulled back to a trot immediately. If your horse is strictly a show horse, you should always try to make him aware that cantering in a buggy is a very undesirable idea, as it is considered a fault in there. However, cantering is a natural gait for horses and sooner or later your horse will break into that gait for one reason or another. It is wise to train him at the canter in a cart once he is driving well to accustom him to the very odd and surging effect of the canter in harness. If you train him, initially with only short bursts of speed, and these only upon YOUR signal, he will not be as prone to become upset and excited when he breaks into a canter by chance later on. In some driving competitions—in timed obstacle work—it is permissible to canter to make up time.

Driving on trails brings to mind picnic lunches and good company and is a great pleasure. With no cars and fewer frightening objects, the driver can relax to a much greater extent and really enjoy the ride. Remember to bring a lunch for your horse, as well as for yourselves, and also his halter and shank. At lunch time, unhitch the horse and put on his halter. It is unwise to tie the horse up while still hitched to the cart. Always check the place where you tie him to ensure that there is no danger of him getting his feet caught in roots or underbrush. As his lunch will have to be fed on the ground, make sure his shank is long enough to reach his feed, but not long enough to get caught. The main thing to watch for while trail driving is to judge the widths of the available spaces accurately while in dense woods. Trails have a trickly habit of narrowing in the worst places, and while carts can negotiate most obstacles, they DO require their own width between objects. If the trail does become too narrow at a certain spot, it is often possible to detour around

Figure 39. H.R.H. The Duke of Edinburgh at the World Driving Championships in 1982 driving H.M. The Queen's Cleveland Bay team. (With permission from H.R.H. and photo by Horse & Driving)

that spot through the woods, but while on this detour, dismount and lead your horse to avoid roots, holes and hidden hazards. Trails also have their complement of steep hills, and when going up or down it is easier on horse and equipment if you dismount and walk beside the cart. Try to avoid stopping the horse in the middle of such a hill. It puts great strain on both his muscles and his training, and he is very tempted to move off to release the pressure and effort. It is a good idea to check your harness occasionally while trail driving as rough going can often cause it to shift or move out of place. Checkreins should be let out much longer or taken off altogether when driving in such country to allow the horse to use his head and neck for greater pulling ability and balance. Long checkreins always remind me of the time I went into a class at the Ottawa Coliseum with a Standardbred whose checkrein I had forgotten to shorten after its previous use out in the country. I touched him up just as we entered the ring to make a good entrance and he put his head down and bucked; that long checkrein let him reach right between his

knees! The buckle on the bellyband must have been weak because it broke and the whole backpad flew up over his head (which was down somewhere between his front and rear legs). There I was, holding the reins of a horse still wearing breastcollar and traces, with his backpad and straps dragging under his front legs. We made several rounds of the ring at an unorthodox gait before I could bring him under control and leave the ring. I have never entered another class since that time without first looking at my checkrein.

It is said that we learn best by experience, but I think it is easier to learn by someone else's experiences — at least it is less painful! However, I am certain that while my readers will always remember to inspect their checkreins and avoid road shoulders at night, over a period of time they will undoubtedly collect many "experience anecdotes" of their own.

HAPPY DRIVING EVERYONE!

Figure 38. Clydesdale Horse to an Antique Cart. Mrs. Glenda Polinder driving "Duke" to win the Ladies Cart Class at the Pacific National Exhibition in Vancouver. Owned by Hollydale Farms, Lyden, Washington.

Figure 40. Six Horse Hitch of Belgians. Consistent champions at all shows, including The Royal Winter Fair. Trained and driven by Jim Poole, Edmonton, Alberta.

References

1. Podhasjsky, Alois, 'The Complete Training of Horse and Rider' — Doubleday and Company Inc. Garden City, N.Y. 1967. P. 47

   Seunig, Waldemar, 'Horsemanship' — Doubleday and Company, Inc. P. 59
2. Walrond, Sally. 'Looking at Carriages' — Pelham Books Ltd. London.
3. Berkibile, Don H. 'Carriage Terminology: An Historical Dictionary' — Smithsonian Institution Press. 1978.
4. Rittenhouse, Jack D. 'American Horse Drawn Vehicles' — Floyd Clymer, Los Angeles, U.S.A.
5. Houghton Buggies, 'The Houghton Sulky Co.' — Marion, Ohio, P.O. Box 502
6. Berkebile, Don H. 'American Carriages, Sleighs, Sulkies and Carts' — Dover Publications, Inc. N.Y.
7. Canadian Equestrian Federation (C.E.F.) — 57 Bloor St. W., Toronto, Ontario, Canada.
8. Ganton, Doris L. 'Drive On — Training and Showing the Advanced Driving Horse.' — Wilshire Book Co. No. Hollywood, Calif. 1982
9. Knight, Captain C. Morley. 'Hints on Driving' — J. A. Allen & Co. Ltd. London, England. 1969.

INDEX

Adjusting harness 7, 9
Appointments 68
Applying whip 28

Backpad 3, 7, 11, 23
Backing up 40, 48, 49, 54
Bending 48
Bits 3, 22
Bit burr 68
Bitting harness 17, 30
Blinkers 3, 7, 9
Boots 22
Brass, cleaning of 64
Breastcollar 3, 9
Breeching 3, 7, 17, 34, 46
Bridle, parts of 3
   adjustment 7, 9
   driving 32
Buggy 51, 59, 65
Buxton bit 68

Carriages, care of 60, 65
Carts 43, 48
Check bit 68
Checkreins 3, 9, 48, 73
Circles 30, 46, 51
Cleaning harness 64
Collars, neck 7
   breast 3
   measuring for 7
Cones 40
Crupper 3, 7, 14, 23
Crupper strap 7, 14

Driving apparatus 24, 27

Elbow bit 68

Figure eights 30, 40, 51, 54
Footman loop 7, 46
Flexion 48
Four-in-hands 76
Free lungeing 32

Gloves 24, 27
Greasing 60
Ground driving 27, 29, 36, 39, 46

Halts 30, 32, 48
Hames 7
Hame tug 7
Hame strap 7
Hands 24, 27, 29, 30, 39, 68
Harness, introduction 23
   cleaning 64
   types of 63, 64

Head set 32
Holding reins 24

Kicking strap 17

Lap robe 76
Length of lessons 22, 40
Line up 68
Liverpool bit 68

Loin strap 7, 14
Long reining 29
Lubrication 60
Lungeing 21

Martingale 9, 32, 48
Mounting 46
Mouthing bit 22

Neck collar 7
Neck muscles 32
Neck strap 9, 11
Noseband 3

Obstacle driving 50

Pads 11
Pair driving 76
Patent leather, care of 64
Poles 35, 36
Ponying 22, 23
Preparation for harness 21

Rein back, ... 40, 49
Rein board 24, 27
Rein guides 76
Reins, side 17, 19
   driving 24, 29, 36
   shortening of 24, 46
Reversing 39, 46, 50, 66
Ring, round 22
   training 2
Running martingale 9, 32

Saddle, back 3, 7, 11
Shaft loops 7, 11, 40
Shafts 45, 51
Shortening reins 24, 46
Side reins 17, 19, 32
Side reining 68
Singletree 3, 11
Ski joring 60
Sleighing 60
Sleigh bells 60
Snaffle, half cheek 3, 68
Splint boots 22
Stops, shaft 14, 45

Tandem driving 76
Teams 76
Thimbles 45
Traces 3, 11, 32, 45
Trace aids 34
Trail driving 79
Training ring 2

Unharnessing 24
Unhitching 48
Unicorn 76

Voice commands 21

Wheels, care of 60
Whip 21, 27, 28
Wrap straps 3, 11, 45

Doris Ganton's
Two-Hour VHS Video Cassette
on
Breaking & Training the Driving Horse

Here is an opportunity to see and hear Doris Ganton discuss many aspects of breaking and training the driving horse. For two hours, you'll receive instructional guidelines that will be extremely useful to you. More than likely, many of the questions you have wanted to ask will be answered. You will enjoy the same valuable information as driving enthusiasts from all over the country who attend Doris Ganton's workshops. You can learn in the privacy of your home.

After watching and listening to the video, you will better understand the fundamentals, procedures, and overall techniques to driving your horse. The tape is sold on a money-back guarantee basis.

Here's how to gain maximum benefit from the video: (1) Watch and listen to the material several times to fully comprehend the practical suggestions and information; (2) Put into practice the specific elements to be incorporated in your breaking and driving program; (3) Evaluate your results; (4) Feel free to write Ms Ganton to discuss your progress and receive suggestions for increasing your proficiency.

Send for Doris Ganton's Two-Hour VHS Video Cassette, Breaking & Training the Driving Horse. Price $75.00 postpaid.

Write and make your check payable to:

Melvin Powers
12015 Sherman Road
No. Hollywood, California 91605